# Contents

# List of Images

## *Introduction*

Just read it. Every word in this document is true, and it is the most important document to ever reach the internet. This document is written to empower good people of the world against the tyranny which exists all around us in our world today. Effectively, the document presented here discloses concealed information about the extent to which medicine, science, and technology has advanced in our **current** era. Moreover, I am disclosing this information because I have been extensively abused, and I am victim of **current** advances in medicine, science, and technology, which I describe in detail below. There are many, many, other victims of abuse, including myself, and therefore it is our plea that you read this document with an open mind and you investigate **ALL** statements which may initially irk you and appear 'suspect' to begin with (the circumstantial evidence is available all around you); because as a victim of abuse, I can honestly say, there is nothing worse than experiencing abuse, and those who have the power to protect you from your abusers, ignore you.

I will now discuss what qualifies as whistle blowing disclosure. After detailing the criteria which qualifies for whistle blowing disclosure, I will detail aspects of the Serious Crime Act, and preface a foundation which defines, explains, and references key information for the reader to understand as well as explore the extent to which medicine, science, and technology has advanced today; all for the express purpose of compelling the reader that medicine, science, and technology, has advanced at an incredible rate; that **current** advances in medicine, science and technology are withheld from public knowledge; and finally these advancements in medicine, science, and technology, have been and are **currently** used to commit **serious unspeakable** crimes against humanity and our environment here on earth. Moreover, it is my aim to present this information as coherently as possible to assist the reader to save me, and save many, many others who experience abuse daily resulting from concealed advances in technology.

## *Whistle Blowing: Qualifying Disclosure*

In the United Kingdom under the Public Interest Disclosure Act (1998) (PIDA) section 43B, a "qualifying disclosure" (whistle blowing disclosure) implies "any disclosure of information which in the reasonable belief of the worker, tends to show one of the following:

a) That a criminal offence has been committed, is being committed or is likely to be committed,
b) That a person has failed, is failing or is likely to fail to comply with any legal obligation to which he is subject
c) That a miscarriage of justice has occurred, is occurring or is likely to occur,
d) That the health or safety of any individual has been, is being or is likely to be endangered,
e) That the environment has been, is being, or is likely to be damaged, or
f) That information tending to show any matter falling within any one of the preceding paragraphs has been, or is likely to be deliberately concealed"

Furthermore, under the Enterprise and Regulatory Reform Act (ERRA) 2013 section 17 (*The new 'public interest' test*) is added for whistle blowing disclosures, amending section 43B of the Employment Rights Act (ERA) 1996 and therefore now reads as such (new words underlined):

"(1) In this part a 'qualifying disclosure' means any disclosure of information which, in the reasonable belief of the worker making the disclosure, *is made in the public interest and* tends to show one or more of the following-- [criminal offence, breach of legal obligation, etc]." (Halliday 2013, p. 2).

The following information is presented **with the express intent** that it is made in the public interest, and meets the all criteria set out in section 43B (a-f) of PIDA as well as the 'public interest test', ERRA section 17. Furthermore, in order for the reader to perceive the credence of my statements, so that (s)he has impetus to research the validity of my statements and not dismiss it as folly supplied by an internet troll who has nothing better to do than waste peoples' time, I will cite the Serious Crime Act 2015 here for the express purpose of convincing the reader that all statements made in this document and my original document are indeed FACTUAL!  THIS IS NO HOAX. THIS IS NO JOKE. This is simply what is happening in the world today.

## *The Serious Crime Act 2015*

The Serious Crime Act 2015 (UK) section 41, 3ZA, amends section 3A of the Computer Misuse Act 1990 which **previously** read [under Computer Misuse Offences]:

### [F1 3A Making, supplying or obtaining articles for use in offence under section 1 or 3

1) [That] A person is guilty of an offence if he makes, adapts, supplies or offers to supply any article intending it to be used to commit, or to assist in the commission of, an offence under section 1 or 3.

To: [The Serious Crime Act 2015, section 41, 3ZA]

**3ZA Unauthorised acts causing, or creating risk of, serious damage**

(1) A person is guilty of an offence if—

    (a) the person does any unauthorised act in relation to a computer;

(2) Damage is of a "material kind" for the purposes of this section if it is—

    (a) damage to human welfare in any place;

    (b) damage to the environment of any place;

    (c) damage to the economy of any country; or

    (d) damage to the national security of any country.

3) For the purposes of subsection (2)(a) an act causes damage to human welfare only if it causes—

    (a) loss to human life;

    (b) human illness or injury;

(4) It is immaterial for the purposes of subsection (2) whether or not an act causing damage—

    (a) does so directly;

    (b) is the only or main cause of the damage.

(5) In this section—

(c)    a reference to a country includes a reference to a territory, and to any place in, or part or region of, a country or territory.

(6) A person guilty of an offence under this section is (unless subsection (7) applies) liable, on conviction on indictment, to imprisonment for a term not exceeding 14 years, or to a fine, or to both.

(7) Where an offence under this section is committed as a result of an act causing or creating a significant risk of—

    (a) serious damage to human welfare of the kind mentioned in subsection (3)(a) or (3)(b), or

    (b) serious damage to national security,

a person guilty of the offence is liable, on conviction on indictment, to imprisonment for life, or to a fine, or to both."

In laymen's terms it is a **serious crime** (Serious Crime Act 2015), punishable by imprisonment, a fine, or both, to cite hatred or spread hoaxes by use of a computer which would cause mass hysteria or public dissension. I have been condemning public figures, high profile individuals, celebrities, singers, movie stars, directors, politicians, world leaders, royalty, anti-secret society 'truthers' (who are really misinformation agents, and agents of deception) etc. –the list is long - since 2011 and **NOT** a single one of these high profile people has issued a public statement saying "I do not like how you have tarnished my name" or filed a law suit against me. Why you may ask? **Because** every word I have stated and will state again (in this document) is true.

## *Fundamentals*

Before I describe the heinous crimes committed against me and many others (including unsuspecting civilians of the world) it is important that I explain, define, and reference:

- Key figures such as Phil Schneider, George Green and Aaron Russo, so that the reader has reference points to verify the extent to which technology has advanced in our **present** era (and continues to advance);
- Define and briefly explain the transhumanist / post human agenda (for those who may be unfamiliar with their aims).
- Define and explain rapid eye movement (R.E.M) sleep, the phases of sleep, and what happens to the (original's) body during sleep.

- Reference advances in technology, with particular attention to: Memory suppression technologies; Mind-voice technology; H.A.A.R.P technology, RFID microchip technology, and MK Ultra technology (CIA's mind control program);
- Define and explain cloning; the different types of clones; cloning centres and cloning technology;
- Define drip feed disclosure / evaluative conditioning and explain why it occurs;
- Explain what 'consciousness transfer' is to the best of my knowledge, and cite drip feed disclosure articles with the express intent to allow the reader to grasp the abuse I have suffered daily at the hands of my tormentors.

## *Key Figures*

### *Phil Schneider*

Phil Schneider (pictured) had 17 years experience working in government black projects carrying a level three security clearance. He was a geologist and engineer who worked in the black projects underground bases at Area 51, S-4, and Los Alamos.

He is most notable for disclosing (Schneider 1995; 1996; Open Minds 2011):

- The 'black budget' expenditure of the United States, which Schneider claims to be between 1.023 trillion U.S. dollars every 2 years ( over $500 billion per year);
- Deep Underground Military Bases (also known as D.U.M.Bs -"dumbs"), and at the time of his lecture (Schneider, 1995), –that there are 131 **active** Deep Underground Military Bases present in the United States, and 1477 Deep Underground Military Bases worldwide;
- Each D.U.M.B costs on average 17-19 billion U.S. dollars; paid for by the taxpayer; and it takes approximately a year-and-a-half to 2 years to build D.U.M.Bs with sophisticated methods.
- That military technology outstrips the general public's technology at a rate of 44 to 45 years of technology for every calendar year which passes. In other words for every 12 months which passes military technology will have advanced by 44 years than what we as the general public is currently accustomed to. Therefore as a rough example if we were to take the year Facebook was founded (2004) as a base year, then the military technology since the creation of Facebook will have outstripped what the

general public is accustomed to by as much as **484 years(!)** (2015 - 2004 = 11. 11 x 44 = 484). Similarly, if we are to use the year which YouTube was founded as a base year (2005), once again, military technology would be 440 years more advanced than what the public is currently accustomed to today.

For the purpose of disclosing current advances in medicine, science and technology, and how such advances are used against me and the people of the world to commit monstrous crimes I will use 1945 as a base year. Everything will become apparent including why I use 1945 as a base year for my disclosure, but for the express purpose of compelling the reader to investigate my disclosure I must present everything, logically, sequentially, methodologically, and provide references for the reader in a coherent way to enable him or her to **pay serious attention** to my eye witness accounts. Therefore, at this present stage keep in mind the year 1945, and the fact that military technology outstrips the general public's technology at a rate of 44 years for every 12 months which passes.

# *George Green*

George Green (pictured) was affiliated with U.S. Presidential candidates, and was once asked to be the Finance Chairman for the next President of the United States. Green would later decline the offer of Finance Chairman when a comment made by Ted Kennedy regarding sleeping with Green's 14 year old daughter caused George Green to re-evaluate his associations with this in-group.

During his 2008 interview with Project Camelot (2008a; 2008b), Green disclosed the following noteworthy information:

- U.S. presidents are "selected" and not elected. This is clearly expressed in a story Green recounts, when Green asks:
  "Who is going to be the next President of the United States [for him to overlook their finances]?"
  And the reply was: "Jimmy Carter"
  Green responds: "Jimmy who?"
  The reply Green received was: "Well, he's the Democratic Governor of Georgia."
  George Green: "But I've been voting Republican."
  Green was then confronted by a tall man, Paul Volcker (American Economist, and Chairman of Federal Reserve under Jimmy Carter and Ronald Regan), who walked over and said, "Son, don't worry about it [Republican or Democrat], we control 'em both."
- U.S. scientists learned how to make people (clones) since 1938 -walking talking ones –and the scientists call these people "synthetics" or "the others".
- Cloning technology is relatively advanced. All that has to be done is take two cells from the original, give the cells a small electrical charge (retain a fertilised egg), then all one needs is a receiver (a womb / artificial womb for the fertilised egg to grow).
- Scientists were excited by the synthetic technology because it meant that spare organ parts could be grown for an "original" human without rejection, because theoretically speaking, the DNA of the synthetic is the same as the original.
- Green gives an example of a cloned Politician: George Walker Bush. Green advices the viewer to seek old video recordings of George W. Bush, and compare the old George W. Bush, with the George W. Bush during Bush's second term,

-in terms of mannerism, speech pattern, body language etc. (old videos of George Walker Bush (Boringest 2006; Fox 4 News - Dallas-Fort Worth 2014) are presented in the References section).

- Scientists have also learned how to make these synthetic people within a few months, to the point where the synthetic can be a walking, talking duplicate of the original, intact with all the memories and experiences of the original. The only problem is that the memory, experiences, and functioning capabilities of these synthetics are like: "A DVD recorder. Sometimes you have glitches, and you have to take the synthetics to Camp David occasionally [every 6 months to a year] to get them tuned up."
- Remember these synthetics are people too, they can think and act just like you can, but they do not have a soul.
- Most of the world leaders have been bought and paid for [by men in the background] and are created to think a certain way –to meet the agendas of these men who remain in the background.
- The global elite plans on depopulating the current human population of **over 7 billion** to **500 million** people. This is corroborated by the "Georgia Guidestones" (WorldTruth 2014).
- Vladimir Putin is executing plans to bring the United States down and into a massive depression. Furthermore, China agrees with Vladimir Putin's plans; stating that the Chinese government has not been a Superpower for over 5000 years and "It is their turn to run the world."
- China has the capacity to set back / shut down all of U.S. computing and electrical systems within two days.

At this present stage, the most **salient** points to keep in mind from Green's accounts are that: U.S. presidents are selected and not elected; and **most importantly**, that scientists have been capable of creating synthetics (cloning people) since 1938. If you have kept in mind Schneider's statement (1995; 1996), (that for every 12 months which passes military technology increases by the equivalent of 44 years compared to what the general public is accustomed to) –then learning that scientists have been capable of cloning humans since 1938 should not come as much surprise. Again, everything regarding my disclosure will become apparent, and I thank these men for disclosing their information, because it helps the reader to corroborate my disclosure.

## Aaron Russo

Aaron Russo (pictured) was an American businessman, director, and political activist. He is best known for directing blockbuster films such as *Trading Places, The Rose* and *Wise Guys*. Russo believed that a human being "Should stand for something, and do the right thing when the time calls to act". Consequently, during the latter part of his career he did his best to warn the American public by producing documentaries such as *Mad as Hell* (1996), *Freedom to Fascism* (Russo 2006), and *Reflections and Warnings* (Jones 2008).

Russo disclosed the following key information in *Freedom to Fascism* (Russo 2006):

## Income Tax

- There is no law requiring Americans to pay income tax. **Although this is a truth, I DO NOT advocate Americans NOT to pay income tax (and neither did Russo).** This is simply because the Federal Reserve can imprison you and seize your possessions for not paying income tax (although there is no law requiring Americans to do so). So for the sake of avoiding hassle for the mean time –pay your income taxes.
- To further illustrate the above point, Bob Shultz speaking at "We the People Foundation" said the following: "Most people believe that the income tax system is legal and that the revenue from the tax is used in the public interest. However, there is a substantial conclusive body of evidence that proves that our income tax system represents the most pernicious form of tyranny. It is the greatest hoax ever perpetrated by government against the working men and women of America."
- Charlie Beall: "The federal government itself refuses to provide, the American people, who are coercively being subjected to this extraction of their private property, without any underlying legal justification. There is no law. There is no law that requires the average American worker in the private sector to pay a direct un-apportioned tax on their labour and compensation for services. There is no law."

- State Representative – Phil Hart –(R-Idaho): "You can look through the statutes, and look for the law that requires you to pay, and when you do that, you **cannot** identify a law that requires the average person in America who earns a wage and works in private business to pay an income tax."
- Peter Gibbons (Tax Attorney) –It's actually very simple. Congress tried to enact an income tax in 1894 –The Supreme Court said that is unconstitutional. When The Supreme Court says something is unconstitutional, it's unconstitutional. They (Congress) tried again in 1913 –and The Supreme Court said –the 16th amendment- "No new power of taxation" –so if they (Congress) didn't have it then (1913) and they didn't get it; they **DON'T** have it. There is no constitutional base for a tax on the wages for Americans living and working in the 50 States of the union. Period. End of argument.

## *Radio Frequency Identification (RFID) Microchips*

- The latest technology for identifying people at the point of self, when they make purchases –is actually the implantable (RFID) microchip. There are microchips that can actually be imbedded directly into human flesh... It's a tiny glass capsule about the size of a grain of rice... it contains an RFID computer microchip with a coiled antenna and it can transmit information also at a distance.
- Katherine Albrecht –Author of "*Spychips*" (2005) makes the following comment: "RFID is a technology that uses tiny computer technology the size of a grain of sand or smaller; hooked up to miniature antennas to transmit information about items at a distance. Back in 1999, Procter and Gamble, Gillette, and MIT got together to find a way to commercialise this technology and make it small enough, make it efficient enough and make it low cost enough to essentially ---their dream is to put these tiny computer chips on every physical item manufactured on planet earth."
- Radio waves can travel through walls, they can travel through wood, and they can travel through things we normally rely on to protect our privacy, for example your purse, your bag-pack, your pocket, –anything you are wearing or carrying.
- One of the most worrisome applications of RFID microchips, are proposals to put them into cash, meaning that it would be able to track every bank note where it had been, who it had been issued to, and create in essence an audit trail. That would essentially take away the anonymity of cash we now enjoy today.
- Once everything you do is tied down to a single number and there is no longer the ability to pay with cash, then all it takes to render you a non citizen is to simply turn that microchip off. **You will no longer be able to participate in any function in society including buying food. Once money becomes digitised through RFID technology, the elite can deduct whatever amount of money they want out of your microchip, whenever they want. They can trace you whenever they want. You will be at their mercy.**

# Habeas Corpus

- Habeas Corpus is "[A] writ [formal document] requiring a person under arrest to be brought before a judge or into court, especially to secure the person's release unless lawful grounds are shown for their detention" (Legal-dictionary 2015).
- During the Bush Presidency [2001-2009 (History 2015)], President Bush signed executive orders giving him sole authority to impose martial law, and suspend Habeas Corpus. This gives him doctorial power over the people without any 'checks and balances.'
  In other words, "The government can jail you for life without charges, without a trial, without a lawyer" (Russo 2006).
- Furthermore: "The National Defense Authorization Act [4] signed by President Obama on the 31st December 2011 authorises the indefinite detention, without trial or indictment, of any US citizens designated as enemies by the executive." See Paye (2013) for further discussion regarding the suspension of Habeas Corpus.

# Fraudulent Manipulation of Election Results

- In 2004, at the "Forum of Presidential Election", Clinton Eugene Curtis, a former Computer Programmer for NASA and ExxonMobil testified under oath that election results can be rigged using electronic programs.
- In 2004, he gave the following abridged testimony (Russo 2006):
  **Judge:** Mr Curtis, are there programs which can be used to secretly fix elections?
  **Curtis:** Yes.
  **Judge:** How do you know that to be the case?
  **Curtis:** Because in October of 2000 I wrote a prototype for present Congressman Tom Feeney, and the company I worked for in Oviedo Florida –it did just that.
  **Judge:** And when you said, "it did just that" –it would rig an election?
  **Curtis:** It would flip the vote 51:49 –whoever you wanted it to go to, and whichever race you wanted to win.
  **Judge:** And would that program that you designed be something that election officials that might be on county boards would actually, could detect?
  **Curtis:** They'd never see it.
  **Judge:** So how would such a program, a secret program that, fixes the election –how could it be detected?
  **Curtis:** You would have to view it either with source code, or you would have to have a receipt and then count the hard paper against the actual vote total –other than that you won't see it.
- **Judge:** Given the availability of such vote rigging software and the testimony that has been given under oath of substantial statistical anomalies and gross differences – between exit polling data and the actual tabulated results, do you have an opinion whether or not Ohio elections, the Ohio Presidential elections was hacked?
  **Curtis:** Yes. I would say it was.

**Person in the audience:** ---So in other words there is absolutely no assurance whatsoever in anything in regard to these machines?
**Curtis:** Absolutely none.

- See Truthstream (2006) for further details regarding the full account of Curtis' testimony on how elections can be manipulated.
- Moreover, voting machine manufactures refuse to allow anyone to see the source code. Without paper ballots, the honesty of any election cannot be verified.

## *The War on Terrorism is the War on Your Freedom*

- It is time to wake up America. These ID cards are not about defeating terrorism, but they are **ALL** about controlling the American people.
- The (mainstream) media controls the information that a person gets in various ways. They can make sure that the average American watching T.V. or reading the newspaper is going to come out with a certain mindset. She is going to say this is good, that's bad –and that is all they (media / elites) have to do.

## *Whoever Makes the Money Makes the Rules*

- As Mayer Rothschild said "Give me control of a nation's money supply, and I care not who makes its laws". Mayer Rothschild, private banker, –knew that he and the other bankers would now control the laws of the nation. Government gave these bankers one of its most important powers, and now had to borrow money from the bankers and pay interest to finance the government.
- America has gone from people owning their own property, owning their own businesses –to a nation in debt because all the money is created by borrowing (from private banks) and this country has become one where people just live by borrowing.

## *Russo's Message to Mankind*

- If you are in the military or law enforcement, remember you swore an oath [to uphold the law of the land]. You did not swear an oath to promote world government, or corporations.
- Now that you do understand what happened [to America, and the monetary system based on debt slavery] and how it is leading to a tyrannical one world government – the future of mankind depends on you –will you choose freedom or slavery?
- Stop being passive liberals. Stop being passive conservatives. Stop being passive centralists. Stop being passive human beings! When the media starts telling you that the country will fall apart if this is done... Do not be fooled!!
- Remember these are sick, malevolent and twisted people we are dealing with, trying to save themselves. Squash their agendas and stay on course.
- "I believe the time for mankind is time to give all or perish. Grow up or die. Grow up and become adults. Act like adults. Take some responsibility. The world which you have perceived is childlike; –and now the curtain has been pulled back for all to see."

- Unless people get active [get fully informed, and learn how governments of the world are conspiring against their people] and say –I am going to help shut down the Federal Reserve System; I am going to shut down the powers that be –the whole human race is doomed otherwise.
- We are coming near the end game and things are starting to accelerate... –and people are looking at the world leaders to declare martial law [which in turn will rid Habeas corpus].

## Let's Consolidate our Problems

- If we can all get focused on how to win the game instead of all these different objectives –such as people are fighting for a better environment; people are fighting to keep their guns / gun control; there are all these different issues which are going on around the world -and which are all important on their own –but if we can consolidate on that and focus –and take all those people –and say –hey let's shut down the Federal Reserve, then we'll deal with those issues. Let's go to the agenda, the objective, the root cause of man's problems, first, then we'll go back to the other stuff.
- That is the priority right now. You have to cut off the head of the beast. And the head of the beast is the Federal Reserve System and the people behind it. You see, and that is what will save the world, and if people understand that –and they **stop** being passive liberals, and **stop** being passive republicans, but rather become **active** human beings –that is what will save the world!

## Aaron Russo: Reflections and Warnings

In this documentary Russo recalls his relationship with Nick Rockefeller. Russo shares critical information Rockefeller discussed with him.

## The Falsehood of September 11th 2001

- Russo met Nick Rockefeller through a female attorney who telephoned Russo and said "One of the Rockefellers would like to meet you." Russo made a documentary called *Mad as Hell* (1996), and Rockefeller had watched the video and knew Russo was running for Governor of Nevada and wanted to meet him. Russo said "Sure I'd like to meet him", and the two met and talked. Rockefeller proved to be a very smart man and shared ideas with Russo and was the person to tell Russo 11 months before 9/11 happened "There was going to be an event..."
- Rockefeller never told Russo what the event was going to be; but, there was going to be an event –and out of that event, we [America] were going to invade Afghanistan, to run pipelines from the Caspian Sea; we were going to invade Iraq, to take over the oil fields and establish a base in the Middle East, and make it all part of the New World Order; and we would go after (Hugo) Chavez and Venezuela –and sure enough, later when 9/11 happened –and I remember he was telling me how you are going to see soldiers looking in caves for people in Afghanistan and Pakistan and all these places and there is going to be this war on terror which has no real enemy and

the whole thing is a giant HOAX, but it is a way for the government to take over the American people (and the world).

- There is no question about it [that 9/11 is a hoax]. Nick Rockefeller said to Russo: "There is going to be a "War on Terror"" and he was laughing. Who are we fighting against...? Why do you think 9/11 happened and then nothing has happened since then? Do you think that our security is so great here that these people who pulled off 9/11, who were able to lock down another plane...? Come on it is ridiculous... 9/11 was done by people in our own government and our own banking system to perpetuate the fear of the American people into subordinating themselves to anything the government wants them to do. That is what it is about; and to create this endless war on terror.

- Nick Rockefeller was laughing when he said, "We are going to be sending men into caves in Afghanistan and Pakistan" –and it was just cynical, he kept laughing and saying "Look how stupid everyone is! We can do whatever we want!"

- 9/11 was the first lie; and the next lie was to go into Iraq, to get Saddam Hussein out with his weapons of mass destruction (when the real issue was control of the oil fields) –that was the next lie. 9/11 created an endless war on terror that would go on and on and you can never define a real winner. There is no one to defeat and so it goes on and on forever. And they can do whatever they want; because they scared the hell out of the American public.

- This whole war on terror is [perpetuated on] a fraud. It is a farce. It is very difficult to say it out loud because people are intimidated in saying it. Because if you say it they want to make you into a nutcase –but the truth has to be... and the truth has to come out. The fact of the matter happens to be the whole war on terror is a fraud, it is a farce. Yes, there is a war going on in Iraq, because we invaded Iraq, and people over there are fighting... but the 'war on terror' –it is a JOKE –you know; and until we discover what really happened in 9/11 and who was responsible for 9/11 –because that is where the war on terror emanates from. That is where it comes from. It was 9/11 which allowed this war on terror to begin and until we get to the bottom root of 9/11 –the truth of 9/11, we'll never know about the war on terror.

- Russo was in Tahiti when 9/11 happened and he got a call from his son –and his son said –"The twin towers, they were just attacked and they are falling down or something..." Russo was in Tahiti and had just woken up from sleep. Russo didn't realise what it was immediately (11 months after Rockefeller had told him about 9/11 and it had happened –because Rockefeller said "There was going to be an event" –he wasn't specific) –but after Russo saw that America was going to go to Iraq and Afghanistan, that is when he realised, and equated it to what Rockefeller had said.

- 9/11 was only a manifestation to create a fear in the American public. So that we would obey and do what they want us to do. Take for example Richard Reed, 'The shoe bomber' –now here is a guy who is 6 feet 6, ugly as can be; I heard he smelled... he sits on a plane, lights a match in a non-smoking area, to put his shoe on fire... surrounded by people... that is idiotic! If you were going to blow up a plane... you would go into the bathroom... you close the door... and you put your shoe on fire...

you are not going to sit there.... surrounded by people, lighting matches in a no smoking flight... they (elite) want you to believe this nonsense. That is ridiculous!

- The war on terrorism is to keep people in fear. It is an endless war without a real enemy ('terrorists') –so that people would submit and do whatever the government wants them to. Submit to searches; give you ID cards; put Radio Frequency Identification (RFID) chips in you etc. You become servants to the elite –that is what this is all about...

- Freedom of liberty is what people really want, and it is time to stop the duplicity of the government from lying to us. You see many people know the truth of what is happening in this country; like 9/11 but they are afraid to stand up. People have to stand up and find their courage and say "I'm not going to take this anymore, I know the truth" –and they create a situation where if you tell the truth, you are considered a lunatic.

- In other words if someone goes on a T.V. show and says that 9/11 was an inside job – immediately the person is labelled an idiot or crazy. They call you names. **You cannot be afraid of that.**

- If you do not fight the corruption and you do not stand up for what is right in life, you end up being a serf and a slave and you are leaving your children a world in which you would not want to live in yourself, so how can you in decency behave that way? You have to stand up for what is right in life, and unless you do that you are nothing.

## *The New World Order Agenda*

- The whole agenda is to create a one world government where everyone has an RFID chip implanted in them. All the money is to be in those chips [a cashless world]. This information came straight from Nick Rockefeller himself. That is what the ultimate plans of the global elite, banking industry and Rockefeller wants to accomplish.

- The agenda is to implant everyone with RFID microchips. All money is transferred to those microchips. There is no more cash. Money would be in microchips. Instead of having cash, you would have money in your microchips, but whenever they want, they (elite) could take whatever amount out of your microchip whenever they want to. Total control. If you are a protestor they just turn off your chip; you cannot buy food; you cannot do anything; it is total control of the people.

- So they want a one world government controlled by them. Everyone being chipped, all the money in those chips, and they control the chips and they control people, and you become a slave. You become a serf to these people –that is their goal. That is their goal; that is their intentions.

- Russo did not believe in enslaving people and Rockefeller would question him in the following manner: "Why do you care about them? Why do you care about those people? What difference does it make to you [Aaron]? Take care of your own life. Do the best you can for you and your family. What do the rest of the people mean to you? They don't mean anything to you. They are just serfs. They are just people..."

- Rockefeller asked –"Why are you fighting for the people for, what is it all about? The people have to be ruled. The constitution, what you are standing for is only for a few people, it's only for a few individuals who can live that way and we believe that it is best for society to be ruled by an elite people who control everything." Russo told Rockefeller he does not believe that. Russo believes: "God put me on this earth to be best person I could be and put everyone on this earth to be the best they can be, and NOT to be a slave and a sheep to YOU and these people (elite) –and I do not understand why you want to control everything. What is the need for that?"
- It was just a lack of caring [from Rockefeller's part], and that is just not who Russo was. It was just sort of like cold you know, and Russo used to say to Rockefeller, "What is the point, of all this? You have all the money in the world you need; you have all the power you need, what is the point? What is the end goal? Rockefeller said "The end goal is to get everyone chipped. To control the whole society. To have the elite people [the bankers and government] controlling the world."

## Women's Liberation from the Perspective of the Elite

- Women's' Liberation was founded by the Rockefellers.
- Rockefeller asked Russo: "What do you think women's liberation was about?" At the time Russo had a pretty conventional thinking about it and he said "It's about women having the right to work; get equal pay with men; just like they won the right to vote." At this point Rockefeller started to laugh and he said to Russo "You're an idiot"
- Rockefeller said –"Let me tell you what that was about. We the Rockefellers funded women's' liberation. We are the ones who got it all over the newspapers and television. The Rockefeller foundation –and you want to know why? There were two primary reasons:"
- 1) "We couldn't tax half the population before Women's Liberation and the second reason was"-
- 2) "Now we get the kids at an early age [because both parents are away from home working] –we can indoctrinate the kids how to think, so it breaks up their family –the kids start looking at the state as the family, as the school as the officials as their family, not as their parents teaching them, and so those are the two primary reasons for women's liberation."
- Russo thought, up to that point, Women's Liberation was a noble thing; however, when he saw the Rockefellers' intentions behind it, where they were coming from when they created Women's Liberation; the thought process of it; Russo saw the evil behind what he thought was a noble venture.

## America is a Republic

- America is a constitution republic / it is supposed to be a constitution republic –and **NOT** a democracy. The majority should not rule, and nor should the majority take over the inalienable rights of the minority.

- Americans pledge allegiance to the "Flag and the **Republic** which it stands" –and **NOT** democracy.
- Democracy is the worst form of government you can have because it is majority rule. Therefore the government can tell you what to do because 'the majority' wants it. It is irrelevant what the majority wants. Decisions should not take away the inalienable rights of an individual.
- Russo also said "It doesn't matter who you vote for, republican or democrat; –they are the same –neither one of them is stopping the Federal Reserve or paying income taxes.
- The elite (Federal Reserve) have taken over the American government; there is no difference between republicans and democrats. There is no difference between the two parties. The duality is manufactured. They (Federal Reserve; central banks) control both parties. It doesn't matter to the elite which one wins, because whoever is running for President will be someone they anoint. Whoever runs for President, will do whatever the elite want them to do. The fact of the matter happens to be that you cannot win an election unless you have enough money to win; they (Federal Reserve; central banks) make sure who gets the money.

## _Depopulation_

- Russo and Rockefeller discussed many things –and one of the things Rockefeller brought up in conversation was reducing the world population. Rockefeller felt that there are too many people in the world. In a way Russo agreed that there are too many people in the world, but he **does not** think he has the authority to say who dies and who lives; but the elite felt that they want to reduce world population and Rockefeller felt it should be reduced by half.
- Rockefeller even mentioned to Russo in conversation, that they were having a real problem trying to solve the Israel / Palestine problem –and they were playing with the idea of bringing Israel to Arizona –and taking everybody from Israel and giving everybody a million dollars, and setting up Israel in the state of Arizona –because that is a problem that they are not in charge of.

## _Borrowing Money from Private Banks causes Inflation and Debt_

- These people (elite) control the money so they make all the rules, and therefore they put the rules in which they want into effect, and the truth is America has really become a socialist communistic country. Everyone says it is a capitalistic country, but how can it be a capitalistic country when you have a central bank? That is the first question people should ask. It can't be. It is a planned economy, it is a phony!
- If they want to create prosperity, they just print dollars, or put digits into the economy. Now you have prosperity. You do not have real prosperity, you do not have real manufacturing; you just have money being injected in, which is infusion of credit. This makes the government go into more debt.

- Whoever makes the money makes the rules. Rothschild said that. Why are we allowing these private bankers to make the money for our country? It is nonsense. Why are we paying interest to these banks to make money for us when the government can do it itself without paying interest, without all that debt? There is no answer to that question and it is a question no politician will raise. Everybody talks about America's debt... We are in debt because we borrow money... but we don't HAVE to borrow money. They designed it so that we can go into debt. We can create the money, and back it by gold so that they cannot create too many of it, so that you do not have the inflation, and do what the Founding Fathers told us.

- Why in the world does the American government borrow money from the banks when they have the ability to create it themselves without borrowing it, and paying interest on it? Why? Nobody can answer that question –not one politician ever raises that. Why does the American government ever borrow money, when they can create it without paying interest?

  –And people say that –well if the American government creates it, it will cause inflation. And that is their answer. And Russo says well let's look at it: the American government has the Federal Reserve do it, which creates the same inflation as if they did it, but also with the inflation –now you are getting massive debt –so with the Federal Reserve you have inflation and debt. Now if the American government made the money, backed by gold, which would limit the amount they could make –you wouldn't have debt and you wouldn't have inflation.

- It wasn't until 1913 when the Federal Reserve came in, that America had inflation. Before then there was no inflation for 100 years. There were points and spikes, mostly during the Civil War –but basically there was no inflation other than during that short period of time. I mean a loaf of bread would cost the same thing. People could plan their lives.

- Today, they have planned inflation, and now you have two parents working, they cannot afford to take and pay for their family anymore; the kids are going to state run schools now, the kids are being indoctrinated how to think; they are being given Ritalin, they are being given all these drugs, the whole country is being dumb down, it is all because of the Federal Reserve System; and the Federal Reserve system and these bankers are responsible for the demise of America. And if we ever want to win this battle you must shut down the Federal Reserve System, and we must shut down these bankers and restore sound money to this country.

- If you analyse the situation and if you realise that since the Federal Reserve has come into being since 1913, illegally, without a constitutional amendment, by bribing a few senators during Christmas vacation, they turned over the most important power that the American government has, the creation and issuance of money to a private bank.

- Through that private bank issuing money they have destroyed this country. They have destroyed the purchasing power of money in this country; they have created social programs that are destroying this country.

- The Federal Reserve has created massive inflation in America which means the American worker has to keep on making more money to keep up with the cost of living. The more money they make to keep up with the cost of living, the less competitive they become in the world economy. So now what happens is that we have to pay our workers so much to keep up with the cost of living; and then they (elite; government; corporations etc.) say screw the American worker, let's go overseas now to get the cheap labour.

- The inflation the Federal Reserve has created has now allowed other countries to outcompete us. Other countries do not have to pay as much money as we have to pay to our workers to survive. So now we are not competitive anymore and we have lost our manufacturing base. We have lost our competitive edge.

- "Freedom to Fascism" is a documentary that everybody should see. Russo and his team show the fraud of the income tax; they show how Judges put people into jail for no reason; they show the corruption of the justice system. They show how the Federal Reserve came into being and how it is controlling society and how all the central banks are working together through the bank of International Settlements, in Switzerland which is the central bank for all central banks and how all are working together to create this one world government; this one world order; which is what they are trying to do.

## *The Deception of the Council of Foreign Relations (CFR)*

- Russo was interested in joining the Council of Foreign Relations, but he found out from Rockefeller himself, that part of the end goal of the CFR is to get everyone RFID chipped. To control the whole society and have the elite people (bankers, government etc.) controlling the world. Russo asked Rockefeller "Do all the people in the CFR believe the way that you do?" Rockefeller said "No, no, no. Most of them believe they are doing the right thing. A lot of them believe it is better off being socialistic. We have to convince people that socialism is really capitalism." Because America is becoming a socialistic country; it is a communist country today.

- Russo's friendship with Rockefeller became one where they would share thoughts, ideas and philosophies and Rockefeller wanted Russo to become a part of what they were doing [enslavement agenda], and for Russo to become a member of the CFR; Rockefeller offered various business opportunities for Russo to get involved in the CFR and to **not** take up the fight or the battle that Russo had been taking up in the past. Rockefeller wanted Russo to drop the idea of helping the people; because "What was the point in Russo fighting for the people?" Rockefeller would question.

- Russo asked Rockefeller: Do all the people of the Council of Foreign Relations feel the same way you feel? Rockefeller said "A lot of them think they are doing the right thing, they think that socialism is the best way to go [but this form of socialism involves redistributing the wealth for the elites and not to everyone], they think that they are doing the right thing. But the people at the [very] top they all know the truth of what is happening." Therefore, the good people in the CFR are also under an illusion, and do not know that effectively they are working for evil men who have the overall goal to control the populace of the world.

- So it is compartmentalised within the elite structure as well. All the people in the CFR, -2000 to 3000 people like Dan Raddler, –they don't know what is going on--- they join the CFR because it is prestigious. They think it is good for business, it is good for this; they don't know what is really happening –the evil that comes out of it –that is emanating out of it.

- In terms of the CFR, in terms of compartmentalisation, there are many good people which Russo believes are part of these organisations who do not even understand what these organisations are really about. For example, when Russo was in Germany, doing cancer treatment, there was a gentleman there who was visiting a friend of his with cancer. The gentleman visiting his friend was a member of the CFR, and him and Russo were talking and Russo showed him the movie (*Freedom to Fascism* (2006)), - and he said, "Oh my god! I'm going to resign." "I had no idea this is what the CFR is about". He had no idea; he is just a nice guy, who thought he was joining a prestigious organisation.

- A lot of people join the CFR because they think it is a prestigious organisation; it will help them in business; make good business contacts etc. They do not have an understanding that the CFR is really about world domination. How they, and the Trilateral Commission, The Bilderberger [Group], the banks, all work together to control the people –a lot of them do not understand that. They do not see the big picture. They think: Oh the CFR is a prestigious organisation. I'll make this, I'll make that, and I can do business deals. It is just business to them. The CFR wants to get the people in there that have influence and power, and so they are part of that (enslavement agenda), and so they are not opposed to them. So the whole country is becoming the haves and the have not. You are getting the very, very wealthy and the middle class being destroyed and you are getting the poor people.

- In Russo's words: "You can call the CFR what you like, but it is a criminal organisation. Run by criminals. But people do not think of it as a criminal organisation, because it has 'class'; 'style'; 'prestige'; –and it is 'respected' -so people do not look at it as being a criminal organisation. That is what a great job they have done."

## *Combining America, Mexico and Canada into one Country*

- Imagine this... here you are in America, and they (elite) are combining American, Canada and Mexico into one country. The North American union. And the American people do not know anything about it. It is not even in the press. They would rather talk about Rosy O'Donnell and Donald Trump calling each other names than discussing the fact that we are merging into one country. This isn't even reported.

- The fact of the matter happens to be, that tells you how controlled the media is. The elite control the media, and they control governments and they are all in bed together. Here you are combining American, Canada and Mexico into one country, and you do not see it in the press. You do not see it in the press. Why? This should be one of the top stories everywhere –and the elite are not worried about it. That tells you –there is the evidence that [media] it is controlled. They do not want the American people to know what is going on, that is why they do not protect our borders. That is why we are losing our constitution, the very document that secures our freedoms.

## *Russo's Vision on How to Bring These People Down*

- There is no question we are in tyranny, there is no question that the American citizen is no longer a free individual human being, to do the things that they wish to do. We're slaves and it is getting worse.
- We are dealing with complete evil; and until the American people wake up and say, we do not want this evil in our country anymore and we want to come back to a country of decency and goodness, integrity and honour, we are going down that road, and that is what it is going to take? It is going to take people to stand up and say we do not want to live in this kind of world anymore. I believe we should pull all of our troops out of Iraq, I believe we should leave other countries alone. Let other countries live their lives the way they choose to. Stop trying to spread 'democracy' around the world, which is the worst form of government there is anyway (because 51 percent rule over 49 percent), restore our republic to what it is supposed to be and go back to what the founding fathers gave us. Restore the republic.
- In Russo's opinion: The populace must shut down the Federal Reserve System –and there has to be an uprising. There has to be an uprising. People have to stand up. One person cannot do it alone. You cannot do it alone. People do not seem to have the courage to do what they have to do.
- A lot of people in Hollywood know the truth, they do not want to stand up and speak about it; I know many of them have seen my movie (*Freedom to Fascism* (2006)) and they know I am right, and they want to talk about it because everybody is afraid. Everybody is afraid because they think that the money they get from the Federal Reserve is really money and they have a comfortable lifestyle and they are afraid of change. They are afraid to stand up for what is right, and until people are willing to stand up and have the courage to do what they need to do, it is not going to change; and hopefully we can affect change when people stand up and say "Hey, I've had enough."
- We (the populace) have one advantage. They (elite) need us to cooperate. See, if we do not cooperate with them, they cannot win. They always need our cooperation with them to go along with their programs. They try to "sell us". Democracy; this majority says this; believe in this; do this, do that; the war on terror; we have to be scared... They are always trying to do things to "sell to us" to go along with them, and once we learn not to cooperate with them; then we win the game.
- That is the point, do not cooperate with them, and do not go along with the program anymore. Stop it. Join forces, and bring freedom back to this country. It is going to take people who believe in freedom; The Constitution and the Founding Fathers, Thomas Jefferson, to make this country whole again, because right now it is in the grip of the evil ones, and the only way to stop that is for good men to stand up.

- We have to stop being scared. We have to do what is necessary to take back what is ours. We have to stop these bankers, these elite, full of liars, congressmen full of liars. They are destroying our borders.
- So through these bankers, attempting to take over America, knowing that America was the freest nation on this earth, it was necessary for them to takeover America, take away gun rights, freedom to bear arms, and create a country where we become slaves, because once they take over America, the rest of the world becomes a lot easier for them. And so by creating 9/11, an event to terrify the American people that we are being 'attacked by terrorist', you create a world where there is an enemy that can **never** be pinpointed. You can never win the battle. It is 100 year war –a never ending war on terrorism. So you are always fighting this war, and through the war on terrorism, through 9/11 which is the first lie, then you create the war on terrorism which is the next lie, then you create the war in Iraq through weapons of mass destruction, which is the next lie –so you get one lie, to the next lie, to the next lie, -- now it is going to be Iran the next lie –and sending more troops and insurgents into Iraq.
- Restore America's Republic back to what it is supposed to be. Get the bankers out of our government. Get government to stop borrowing money from the banks. Government should make its own money; restore the Republic. Restore individual freedoms. That is what this country is about -and until we do that we are going to be slaves.
- You have to take away the creation of money away from the private bankers and you will solve 95% of your problems.
- Americans, mobilise, stand tall, stand together, and tell the government you are "Mad as hell!" Do not cooperate with the government do not accept a National ID card. Do everything in your power to restore freedom and your individuality back to America. Stop being a country run by the institutions for the institutions. Let's go back to "We the people, by the people for the people", as opposed to, we the institutions, by the institution, for the institution. Stand up for your individual rights. Stand up for the God leaders that are in each and every one of us!

## *The Trans-humanist / Post Human Agenda*

Transhumanism is a cultural and intellectual movement that believes we can, and should, improve the human condition through the use of advanced technologies. One of the core concepts in transhumanist thinking is life extension: through genetic engineering, nanotech, cloning, and other emerging technologies, eternal life may soon be possible. Likewise, transhumanists are interested in the ever-increasing number of technologies that can boost our physical, intellectual, and psychological capabilities beyond what humans are naturally capable of (thus the term *trans*human) (Anthony 2013). Transcranial direct current stimulation (tDCS), for example, which speeds up reaction times and learning speed by running a very weak electric current through your brain, (Anthony 2012) has already been used by the US military to train snipers. On the more extreme side, transhumanism deals with the concepts of mind uploading (to a computer), and what happens when we finally craft a computer with greater-than-human intelligence (the technological singularity) (See: "How to create a mind, or die trying", Hewitt 2012) (Anthony 2013).

Moreover, put simply, "posthumanism" can be defined as that condition in which humans and intelligent technology are becoming increasingly intertwined (TheNanoAge 2015). For readers interested in learning more about the posthuman / transhuman agenda, see BT Soul Catcher 2025 (BEAMS 2007); Avatar Project 2045 (2045 Initiative 2015; Borghino 2012) and Mind Clone Robot (Bloomberg Business 2015; RT 2015) which have all been disclosed as methods of transferring the human consciousness to a computer.

## *The Phases of Sleep and Rapid Eye Movement (R.E.M) Sleep*

Sleepers pass through five stages of sleep: 1, 2, 3, 4, and REM (rapid eye movement) sleep. These stages progress cyclically from stage 1 through REM then begin again with stage 1. A complete sleep cycle takes an average 90 to 110 minutes (Sleepdex 2015). In other words, after falling asleep, it takes approximately 90 to 110 minutes to enter REM sleep.

Stages

| Waking | REM Sleep | NREM Sleep | | | | |
|---|---|---|---|---|---|---|
| | | Light Sleep | | Deep Sleep | | |
| Stage 0 | Stage R | Stage 1 | Stage 2 | Stage 3 | Stage 4 | |
| Eyes open, responsive to external stimuli, can hold intelligible conversation | Brain waves similar to waking. Most vivid dreams happen in this stage. Body does not move. | Transition between waking and sleep. If awakened, person will claim was never asleep. | Main body of light sleep. Memory consolidation. Synaptic pruning. | Slow waves on EEG readings. | Slow waves on EEG readings. | |
| 16 to 18 hours per day | 90 to 120 min/night | 4 to 7 hours per night | | | | |

Image 1: Stages of sleep. Source: Sleepdex: (2015)

**Any sufficiently advanced technology is indistinguishable from magic.**
**Arthur C. Clarke**

## *REM Sleep*

Most dreaming occurs during Stage Five, known as REM. REM sleep is characterized by eye movement, increased respiration rate, and increased brain activity. REM sleep is also referred to as paradoxical sleep because, while the brain and other body systems become more active, your muscles become more relaxed, or paralyzed. Dreaming occurs because of increased brain activity, but voluntary muscles become paralyzed. Voluntary muscles are those that you need to move by choice, for example, your arms and legs. Involuntary muscles are those that include your heart and gut. They move on their own (Sleepdex 2015; Walcutt 2013).

Rapid eye movement, or REM sleep, is when you typically dream. You may have images float by in earlier stages, particularly when you are going through Alpha or Theta (brain waves), but the actual dream state occurs in REM (Walcutt 2013).

This period of paralyzation is a built-in protective measure to keep you from harming yourself. When you are paralyzed, you can't leap out of bed and run. Do you ever feel like you can't escape during a dream? Well, the truth is, you can't. You can breathe, and your heart is working, but you really can't move (Walcutt 2013).

The reader is also advised to see the Horizon documentary "Why Do We Dream?" (BBC Horizon 2009). This video is available, on YouTube, and details sleep, the phases of sleep, REM sleep, the period of paralysation and more.

## *Current Advances in Technology*

This is a section some readers may have difficulty with, because reading about these current technologies alone, one cannot help but feel that such technologies described below sound like the stuff of science fiction and fantasy, although they have been corroborated through public drip-feed disclosure (explained below). Nevertheless, I urge the reader to keep in mind Arthur C. Clarke's quote (above), as well as Phil Schneider's testimony regarding the advancements of military technology in comparison to the general public's technology (for every 12 months, military technology outstrips the technology the public is accustomed to by a rate of 44 years). Moreover, for the reader who finds difficulty understanding the technologies described below, seek the supporting articles / videos.

## Memory Suppression Technologies

Memory suppression technologies are any scientifically advanced technologies which are used to suppress memory. Examples of how memories can be suppressed can be found by reading Winter's (2014) article which details how memories can be suppressed using light; and Greenberg's (2013) article which discusses memory suppression through gene / chemical modification.

## Mind-Voice Technology

Mind-voice technology is an advanced technology which is capable of reading, listening, hearing or broadcasting your inner voice / thoughts. Examples of articles which discuss mind-voice technology are: Prigg (2014) details software which can read the inner voice; and New Scientist (2014) which also discusses a brain decoder which can eavesdrop on one's inner voice.

## H.A.A.R.P. Technology

The High frequency Active Auroral Research Program (HAARP) is a radio transmitting system that can bounce signals off the ionosphere (a region of the Earth's upper atmosphere 60km (37 miles) to 1000km (620 miles) altitude) and back to earth to probe deep into the earth or sea, its proponents say. The system could locate minerals or communicate with submarines (Begich & Manning 1997; Sheen, Begich & Robbins 2005).

HAARP can also:

- Disrupt human mental processes.
- Knock out all global communications systems.
- Manipulate global weather.
- Change weather patterns over large areas.
- Interfere with wildlife migration patterns.
- Hurt ecosystems.
- Negatively affect your health, moods, and mental states.
- Unnaturally impact the Earth's upper atmosphere.

This illustration (below) shows the ionosphere's relationship to the Earth. The illustration appeared in the HAARP Environmental Impact Statement on page 10-125 of Volume II.

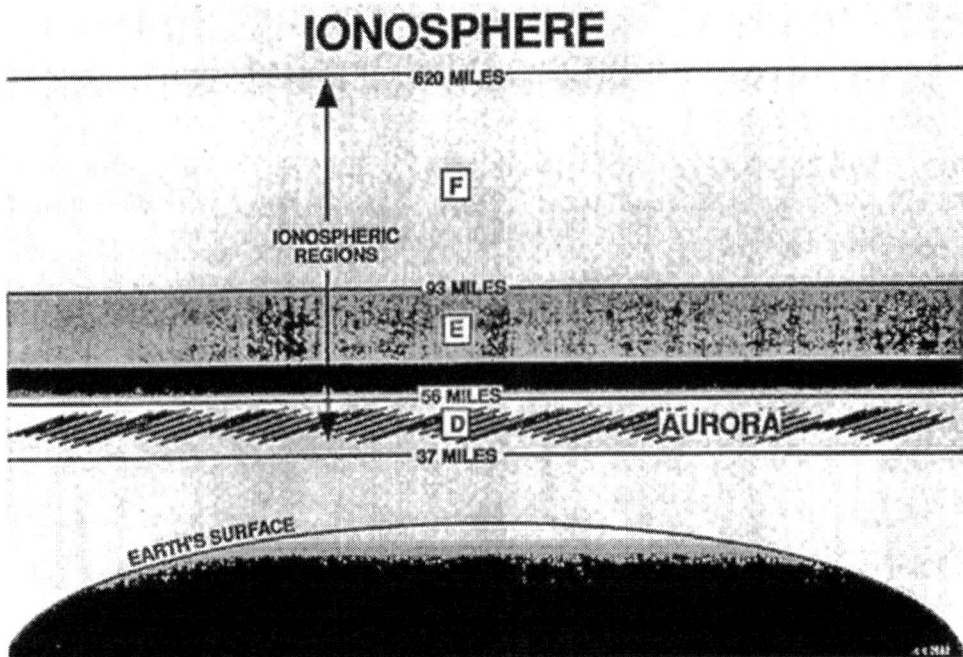

**Image 2: The ionosphere's relationship to earth. Source: (Begich & Manning 1997)**

The ionosphere protects the earth. HAARP (High frequency Active Auroral Research Program) is made to beam more than 1.7 gigawatts (billion watts) of radiated power into the ionosphere -the electrically charged layer above Earth's atmosphere. Put simply, the apparatus is a reversal of a radio telescope -just transmitting instead of receiving. It will boil the upper atmosphere. After disturbing the ionosphere, the radiations will bounce back onto the earth in the form of long waves which penetrate our bodies, the ground, and the oceans.

HAARP represents a technology which could lead to a new class of weapons that could change our world profoundly -an all-purpose military tool. If misused, the tool could mess up the weather. It could be used against humanity in a way that would change what people think, believe and feel. It could be used for good or evil, just as a harp can produce the music of Mozart or the melody of a death march.

## *H.A.A.R.P. and Weather Control*
- "The theoretical implication [of Dr. Robert Helliwell and John Katsufrakis of Stanford University in 1974] suggested by their work is that global weather control can be attained by the injection of relatively small 'signals' into the Van Allen belts (radiation belts around Earth) -something like a super-transistor effect" said Frederic Jueneman.
- Yes. The weather can be controlled using HAARP technology.

- A series of weather disasters began in 1960, according to a CIA report mentioned in the editorial, but at the time climatologists couldn't look ahead and see that droughts, floods and abnormal temperatures would continue beyond that decade. As if natural disasters weren't bad enough, the CIA reported that national governments were already able to manipulate weather for military purposes [using HAARP technology].

As far back as 1958, the chief White House advisor on weather modification, Captain Howard T. Orville, said the U.S. Department of Defence (DoD) was studying ways to manipulate the charges of the earth and sky and so affect the weather by using an electronic beam to ionize or deionize the atmosphere over a given area. In 1966, Professor Gordon J. F. MacDonald, associate director of the Institute of Geophysics and Planetary Physics at the University of California, Los Angeles, was a member of the President's Science Advisory Committee, and later a member of the President's Council on Environmental Quality.

Gordon J. F. MacDonald published papers on the use of environmental control technologies for military purposes. MacDonald made a revealing comment: —The key to geophysical warfare is the identification of environmental instabilities to which the addition of a small amount of energy would release vastly greater amounts of energy. MacDonald had a number of ideas for using the environment as a weapon system and he contributed to what was, at the time, the dream of a futurist. When he wrote his chapter, —"How to Wreck the Environment" for the book "Unless Peace Comes" he was not kidding around.

In the text, MacDonald describes the use of weather manipulation, climate modification, polar ice cap melting or destabilization, ozone depletion techniques, earthquake engineering, ocean wave control and brain wave manipulation utilizing the planet's energy fields. He also said that these types of weapons would be developed and, when used, would be virtually undetectable by their victims. He was not some wire haired fanatic when he made these observations in 1966, -he had the credentials of a world recognized scientist. What his futuristic concepts became, are the things which projects like HAARP are made of...

## *H.A.A.R.P. and Mind Control*
- Radio frequency radiation, acting as a carrier for extremely low frequencies (ELF), can be used to wirelessly entrain (adjust) brain waves.
- We are talking about very, very, low power requirements. The trick for influencing brain activity is in the combination of frequency, power level and wave form.
- As Dr. Patrick Flanagan, one of America's most gifted inventors noted in an interview, the HAARP project could be not only the biggest ionospheric heater in the world, but also the biggest brain-entrainment (brain adjustment) device ever conceived.
- According to HAARP records, when the device is built to full power it can send very low frequency (VLF) and extremely low frequency (ELF) waves using many wave forms at energy levels sufficient to affect the mental states of entire regional populations.

- The HAARP transmitting system could be used unintentionally or intentionally to alter mental functions.
- If HAARP is tuned to the right frequency, using just the right wave forms, mental disruption throughout a region could occur intentionally or as a side effect of the radio frequency transmissions [in other words: "mind control"].

## RFID Technology

Radio Frequency Identification (RFID) microchips are microchips that can be directly imbedded into human flesh. This section discusses the dangers of RFID chips. See Rense (2001) for full review.

- RFID technology links the brains of people via implanted microchips to satellites controlled by ground-based super-computers.
- Today they are small enough to be inserted into the neck or back, and also intravenously (through a vein) in different parts of the body during surgical operations, with or without the consent of the subject. It is now almost impossible to detect or remove them.
- Implanted human beings can be followed anywhere.
- Today's microchips operate by means of low-frequency radio waves that target them. With the help of satellites, the implanted person can be tracked anywhere on the globe.

## RFID Technology and the Medical Profession

- One reason the dangers of implantable microchip technology has remained a state secret is the widespread prestige of the psychiatric DIAGNOSTIC STATISTICAL MANUAL IV produced by the U.S. American Psychiatric Association (APA), and printed in 18 languages. Psychiatrists working for U.S. intelligence agencies no doubt participated in writing and revising this manual. This psychiatric "bible" covers up the secret development of Mind Control technologies by labelling some of their effects as symptoms of paranoid schizophrenia.
- The Psychiatric Diagnostic Statistical Manual (DSM) for mental disorders has been a brilliant cover up operation in 18 languages to hide the atrocities of military and intelligence agencies' actions towards their targets. THE MANUAL LISTS ALL MIND CONTROL ACTIONS AS SIGNS OF PARANOID SCHIZOPHRENIA.
- If a target is under surveillance with modern technology via TV, radio, telephone, loudspeakers, lasers, microwaves, poisoned with mind altering drugs via air-ducts, giving familiar smells which cause headache, nausea and so forth, if s/he claims her/his clothes are poisoned, her/his food or tap water as well ---all medical schools teach their students that the person is paranoid, ESPECIALLY if s/he believes intelligence agencies are behind it all.
- Never is the medical profession told that these are routine actions all over the world by intelligence agencies against their targets. Thus, victims of mind control are falsely considered mentally ill and get no help since they are not believed and their suffering is doubled by misinformed health professionals.

## Further Implications of RFID Technology

- How many people realize what the implications of implantable chips actually mean? It means total loss of privacy and total outside control of the person's physical body functions, mental, emotional and thought processes, including the implanted person's subconscious and dreams! For the rest of his / her life!

- It sounds like science fiction but it is secret military and intelligence agencies' mind control technology, which has been experimented with for over half a century (since 1950s). Totally without the knowledge of the general public and even the general academic population.

- Supercomputers in Maryland, Israel and elsewhere with a speed of over 20 BILLION bits/sec can monitor millions of people simultaneously. In fact, the whole world population can be totally controlled by these secret brain-computer interactions, however unbelievable it sounds for the uninformed.

- Neuro-electromagnetic involuntary human experimentation has been going on with the so-called "vulnerable population" for over 50 years, in the name of "science" or "national security" contrary to all human rights. It happens today in the **USA, Japan, and Europe**. With few exceptions, the mass media suppresses all information about the entire topic.

- Only increased public awareness of the microchip implants, their frightful consequences to privacy by influencing of individuals' thoughts and actions, causing people to become biological robots with physical and emotional pain whenever the supercomputer technician so wishes, is enough reason to refuse to take the microchip into your body for whatever reason.

- It is the biggest threat to humanity and the most sinister plan to enslave the human race forever.

If you have a choice and want to remain a normal human being with privacy, **DO NOT** have your children implanted **NOR** yourself implanted with RFID microchip(s) or any other type of implantable microchip. Otherwise your vision, hearing, sensing, thoughts, dreams and subconscious will be influenced by an outsider, who does not have your best interests in mind. For the rest of your life!

## Mind Control: MK Ultra Technology

MK Ultra today has evolved from the 1950s variation of mind control (MK Ultra Compendium 1980), whereby drugs such as LSD, and interrogation were used as methods to weaken the mind of the individual to force confessions through mind control. Today, mind control is achieved through the implantable microchip (mentioned above; Rense 2001).

- The brain functions of an implanted person can then be remotely monitored by supercomputers and even altered through the changing of frequencies.

- Once implanted, the U.S. National Security Agency's (NSA) 20 billion bits / second supercomputers could now "see and hear" what you are experiencing with a remote monitoring system (RMS).

- Every thought, reaction, hearing and visual observation causes a certain neurological potential, spikes, and patterns in the brain and its electromagnetic fields, which can now be decoded into thoughts, pictures and voices. MK Ultra technology is therefore capable of Mental Video and Audio Projection, as well as Artificial Telepathy.
- The mass media have not reported that an implanted person's privacy vanishes for the rest of his or her life. S/he can be manipulated in many ways. Using different frequencies, the secret controller of MK Ultra technology can even change a person's emotional life. S/he can be made aggressive or lethargic. Sexuality can be artificially influenced. Thought signals and subconscious thinking can be read, dreams affected and even induced, all without the knowledge or consent of the implanted person by using MK ultra technology.
- Memory suppression technologies are used in conjunction with MK Ultra technology, which enables the programmer to control certain memories the victim remembers. The use of memory suppression technologies and MK Ultra technology allows the programmer to reinforce behaviour and elicit specific conditioned responses.
- Mind control techniques, such as MK Ultra, can be used for political purposes. The goal of mind controllers today is to induce the targeted persons or groups to act against his/her own convictions and best interests. Zombified individuals can even be programmed using MK Ultra technology, to murder and remember nothing of their crime afterward.
- The goal of mind control, using MK Ultra technology is to program an individual to carry out any task against their will and self-preservation instinct and to control the absolute behaviour and thought patterns of the individual. The purpose of mind control, using MK Ultra technology is to disrupt memory, discredit people through unusual behaviour, to make them insane or to commit suicide or murder.

See Mind-Computer (2012) which discusses how artificial telepathy is achieved. Artificial telepathy, also known as 'brain to brain communication', is possible using MK Ultra technology. Furthermore, review: Jim Cristea (2009); Berkeley News (2011); UC Berkeley Campus Life (2011) CTForecaster (2013); nature video (2013) and Stromberg (2013). The above mentioned articles and videos describe, demonstrate, and corroborate how audio and video projection of the brain is achieved; how dreams can be recorded and projected digitally; how the brain can be scanned to reveal hidden information personal to an individual; and what a person's underlying intentions are, by using brain scans. Moreover, the articles and videos mentioned above confirm the functionalities of MK Ultra technology.

Furthermore, when our brain functions are connected to supercomputers by means of RFID technology, MK Ultra technology and other implantable microchips, it will be too late for protest. This threat can be defeated only by educating the public, using available literature on biotelemetry (electronic equipment that receives signals from radio transmitters) and information exchanged at international congresses.

# _Human Cloning_

There are currently five different types of clones, concealed from public knowledge. There are Mark 1 clones; Mark 2 Clones; Mark 3 Clones; and Mark 4 clones and reanimated clones. Moreover, there are two types of cloning techniques: duplication cloning and replication cloning.

Mark 1 clones are REM sleep driven clones. However, the technology used for Mark 1 clones causes many side effects and therefore Mark 1 REM sleep driven clones are no longer a preferred choice.

Mark 2 clones are also REM sleep driven clones. Mark 2 clones have fewer side effects than Mark 1 clones, and therefore Mark 2 clones are currently the preferred method for REM sleep driven clones.

Mark 3 clones are independent clones which operate on microchip containing the entire consciousness of an individual.

Mark 4 clones are also independent clones, operating on a microchip which contains the entire consciousness of an individual and is an advanced version of a Mark 3 clone.

These independent clones (Mark 3 and Mark 4) have a lifespan of 6 months to 12 months and require adjustments after this period to run efficiently once more. Without these adjustments, their functionality weakens.

To "reanimate" means "to restore to life; resuscitate; revive". Consequently, reanimated clones are clones which are genetically identical to that of a person who once lived.

Replication cloning is what the public is most familiar with. Replication cloning involves giving birth to a genetic identical of an original where the newborn starts life off as a baby and matures. The newborn is referred to as a clone.

However, duplication cloning is a current concealed advanced from of cloning, and it involves taking as little as two cells from an individual, adding a constant electrical charge to the cells until a complete human being is formed.

Duplication cloning is similar to the process of regenerative medicine as demonstrated by Dr. Stephen Badylak's video "How to grow a New Fingertip" (CBS 2008; Science Channel 2014) where Badylak states: 'A whole human can be grown within 9 months.' On average it takes 5 months to grow a duplicate clone of an original by means of advanced scientific and technological regenerative procedures.

## Cloning Centre and Cloning Technology

A cloning centre is a place where clones are produced. Cloning technology are the advancements in medicine, science and technology used to produce duplicate and replicate copies of originals.

## Drip Feed Disclosure and Evaluative Conditioning

### Drip Feed Disclosure

Drip feed disclosure is the process of supplying information but in small amounts overtime. Drip feed disclosure is also the process of revealing information slowly overtime, possibly telling lies to conceal certain aspects of the truth until the source administering the drip feed disclosure has adequate time to let out the truth in a slow and controlled way, thereby delaying the betrayed partner (in this disclosure, the public) from having the "complete truth" for some time.

Drip feed disclosure is also a method to gauge public reaction used by governments, the media, multinational corporations and organisations as well as high ranking officials to "test" whether the general public is acceptant of the concealed information or not. When the public reacts favourably to the drip feed disclosure, more information is revealed and made public, and it appears to the unsuspecting observer that the people involved in making the disclosure are taking positive steps towards a favourable goal for all. However, when the public reacts adversely; information contradicting the drip feed disclosure is presented, and an expert is presented to the public who voices the concerns of the general public, and therefore it appears that the opinions of the public have been noted and research and development will not continue in the initial stated direction. Nevertheless, the truth remains concealed and research and development continues despite the aversions of the public.

Examples of drip feed disclosure involve articles such as mind uploading / downloading (BEAMS 2007), Mind Clone Robots (Bloomberg Business 2015; RT 2015), The 2045 Avatar Project (2045 Initiative 2015; Borghino 2012). I am here to tell you that I have been a spy for over 30 years and such technological accomplishments which are posted under trans-humanism / post-humanism genre have been realised many years ago and are **available** today. They are just concealed from the public.

Furthermore, Dolly the sheep was announced as the first publicly cloned mammal (Animal Research 1996), but how many readers can say they know that, four years later, a monkey (BBC News 2000), our closest primate, was cloned? This is publicly disclosed knowledge, but I suspect that not many people are aware of a monkey being cloned four years after Dolly. This is because there was such a worldwide adverse reaction to genetic cloning when Dolly was made public, that the disclosure of the cloned Rhesus monkey (BBC News 2000) was not made public knowledge on a grand scale.

## _Evaluative Conditioning_

_Evaluative conditioning_ is defined as a change in liking, which occurs due to an association with a positive or negative stimulus (see De Houwer et al., 2001). Simply put, this means that our preferences for brands, products, people and other things can be influenced and even modified by the presence of something we like or dislike strongly (Hale 2012).

In many settings, a neutral stimulus, called a "conditioned stimulus", often coincides with some desirable or undesirable object, called the unconditioned stimulus. An unknown brand, for example, might appear in a commercial that also depicts a happy child. Over time, stimuli that often coincide with desirable objects are perceived more favourably, whereas stimuli that often coincide with undesirable objects are perceived less favourably--called evaluative conditioning (De Houwer, Thomas, & Bauyens, 2001; Walter, Nagengast, & Trassilli, 2005; Moss 2009). An "unconditioned response" is a response to a neutral stimulus we have no / little control over. It is a natural automatic response.

In other words, our preferences for liking or disliking brands, products etc. (the neutral stimulus) can be influenced by embedding (implicitly placing) the brand etc. (neutral stimulus) with positive or negative associations. Overtime our conditioned response becomes one of conditioned favourable or negative response towards the brand, product etc. (neutral stimulus) when we are faced with the brand, product etc. at a future date. Our preferences have been guided overtime. Evaluative conditioning can change our preferences when carried out subliminally or implicitly; it does not have to be explicit.

In media; music; movies; and other forms of popular culture and entertainment, images and symbols (of stimuli which cause undesirable consequences) are embedded subliminally and implicitly and are paired with positive associations as a form of evaluative conditioning. This causes individuals who have no preconceived judgements of the stimulus to be guided to have positive associations with a stimulus which causes undesirable consequences.

In popular culture; media; advertisements; movies; music and other forms of entertainment, evaluative conditioning is used as a method of hinting (that something is wrong); showing off of power (i.e. nothing can be done to stop the negative stimulus) and as a form of gloating (i.e. we've pulled off the negative stimulus / we are pulling it off). In over the 30 years I have been a spy, I have witnessed methods of evaluative conditioning used to hint, show off power, and gloat more often than not, and evaluative conditioning is not used just to guide social order.

The fortunate aspect is that once a person learns that his / her preferences are being guided by methods of evaluative conditioning, in order to influence the person to have positive associations with negative stimuli (or feel powerless towards the negative stimuli); and that the stimulus (brand / product) does in fact cause undesirable consequences –then the 'spell' is broken. The person can now choose how he or she responds to the brand etc. Usually, once all is known: a negative stimulus is associated with negative associations; despite it being portrayed as positive through evaluative conditioning.

## *Consciousness Transfer*

Consciousness is defined as "the state of being aware of and responsive to one's surroundings; a person's awareness or perception of something" (Dictionary Reference 2015). Consciousness can also be described as: individual awareness of a person's unique thoughts, memories, feelings, sensations and environment (Cherry 2015).

John Locke (1632-1704) was an English philosopher, Oxford academic and medical researcher who argues that it is sameness of consciousness rather than sameness of substance that constitutes personal identity. Consequently, if the psychological life is transferred from the body of a prince to the body of a cobbler (shoe mender), Locke argues, the resulting person will be the prince and not the cobbler. He would be responsible for the prince's actions and not the cobbler's; those who were close to the prince could continue their relationships with him but those who had relationships with the cobbler could not, and so on (Schechtman 2012, p.334). Moreover, basic Lockean intuition has proved to be that "consciousness transfer" can be thought of as the feat in which the person moves from one body into another (Schechtman 2012, p.334).

Consciousness transfer can also be thought of as the process of transferring or copying the mental content (including long-term memory and "self") from a particular brain and copying it to a computational device; artificial body or avatar body such as that of a robot or clone version of the original. The computation device, robot or the clone, will then respond essentially the same way as the original brain (as suggested by Lockean theory on consciousness transfer) and therefore the computational device, robot or clone experiences having a conscious mind and essentially the behaviour of the computational device, robot or clone, can be attributed as belonging to that of the original.

It is **OF MONUMENTAL IMPORTANCE** that the reader understands the above statement regarding consciousness transfer is a method of **CURRENT** concealed advances in technology and not a concept relegated only to the genre of science fiction. At the very least the reader should be **open** to the possibility of consciousness transfer and the implications of consciousness transfer, in order to truly begin to understand the extent to which current concealed advances in technology are used to commit monstrous crimes.

I understand the above sounds unsettling, but there are also many wonderful concealed advances in technology (detailed in the disclosure section). The marvels in technological feats and human accomplishment will be released for the benefit of mankind once the world learns about the monstrous crimes which are committed against the them, and the earth, through the use of highly concealed technological advances, and the good people of the world band together to put an end to the tyranny around us.

Now is also a good time to remind the reader that if military technology advances by a rate of 44 years for every 12 months which passes, then since 1945 military technology has advanced by a rate of more than 3000 years compared to the technology the public is currently accustomed to (44 times 70 = 3080). Now ask yourself honestly, in 3000 years from now (the year is 5015) don't you think humans will have been capable of developing a method which allows them to transfer their consciousness from one body to the next and more?

I am here to tell you that I have been a spy for over 30 years and that from the intelligence I have gathered over the years it has been illustrated to me countless times that consciousness transfer is indeed fact and currently exists. Consciousness transfer has been achieved since 1945, although this accomplishment in human advancement (and more) is concealed from public knowledge. Moreover, consciousness transfer is a highly advanced form of concealed technology used by high ranking members of society to commit unspeakable crimes against the public.

Furthermore, for the reader who wishes to understand how consciousness transfer is possible, see Petkova and Ehrsson (2008) and Ehrsson (2013). In the video Professor Henrik Ehrsson (2013) demonstrates:

1) Consciousness transfer from one body to the next (owning another body other than ones original)
2) Physiological evidence for owning the new body. In other words when consciousness has been transferred and the person perceives the new body as that of his or her own; when the new body is threatened as the mannequin (new body) was in the experiment, individuals still perceived the mannequin body as that of their own and became frightened (displayed biological and physiological responses).
3) Visual perception and stimulation causes us to perceive ownership of a new body.
4) The new body we inhabit must be similar to that of our own (it does not matter whether the new body is smaller or larger than our original so long as the measurements are proportional) for consciousness transfer to occur.

5) That it is possible for consciousness to be transferred to another person's body and have (or perceive) ownership of other person's body while being localised in your own body. In other words, dual consciousness is possible.

Petkova and Ehrsson's (2008) and Ehrsson's (2013) research gives one of the clearest publicly disclosed explanations of consciousness transfer and I urge the reader to watch the video in order to better understand my disclosure. One of the main findings from his research is that perception is not rigid; and perception does shape reality. Sight and synchronous (going on at the same time) stimulation can, and does alter the brains perception of reality. Sight and synchronous stimulation activates certain parts of the brain (the sensory parts of the brain and the motor (movement) parts of the brain). The match between the two (sight and stimulation) "convinces" the brain that 'hey, I'm no longer in this body; I'm in that one or that I have a third arm (although it is a false limp) etc. Accordingly, "perception is reality".

## *Disclosure: Save the Victims through your Diligence*

I've done my best to preface this information as logically, sequentially and methodologically for the reader as possible. I have stated what the law is on 'whistle blowing'; I have given references and definitions where appropriate and I have provided many sources in order for the reader to research, corroborate, and better understand my disclosure, so that he or she becomes compelled to help me and victims like me, defeat tyranny and save the future of mankind; therefore if there are any areas of my disclosure which still appears suspect –and I understand, after all my efforts –things may still not appear clear to some readers because we are dealing with highly advanced concealed technologies which are not available in the world the general public lives in; and therefore it is difficult to fathom and furthermore conceive that men can be so evil to their fellow humans through the use of advances in science and technology. Nevertheless, I promise you, I have no reason to lie, I am victimised daily because of these technologies, and therefore my only option is to tell the truth, and nothing but the truth so that the people of the world can put an end to this grave injustice.

For the reader who still finds it difficult to accept my disclosure after first read, I want you to do two things:

1) **Give me the benefit of the doubt.** I am asking you to do this because as I stated earlier, one of the hardest things to do as a victim of abuse is to come forward about the abuse one has suffered. It is even more heartbreaking when nobody believes you. Consider all the victims of paedophiles you have heard about on the news. I cannot speak for their individual cases but I can attest to the fact it affects my mental psyche beyond comprehension; there is nothing worse than being ignored and that nobody believes you. So on that premise, please give me the benefit of the doubt, because I'm sure the majority of good human beings out there will feel worse when it is proven that I am a victim of severe abuse and you ignored me, when you could have done everything in your power to save me.

2) **Set out on a genuine quest to debunk my disclosure.** If my disclosure appears suspect to you to begin with, then set out on a genuine and investigative quest to debunk my disclosure because, if my disclosure initially appears circumspect to believe, then I should be proven false within minutes of your research of my disclosure, because even professionals make mistakes. There will be something about the disclosure which will just not 'add up'. However, when a person is telling the truth, then it is very difficult to debunk that person.
I promise you, it will be worth your time to know the real truth about the world, simply because the truth is liberating.

I would also like to remind you that the truth about the world has been hidden from the public for many decades, therefore when you do hear the truth of course it is going to sound absurd to begin with; but keep an open mind and pursue till you know what truth is; because "to "know" is to understand with certainty".

## *Words of Inspiration: Personalized from a Theoretical Physicist –Thomas Campbell*

The following gives an introduction to many aspects which occur in this world behind closed doors or in plain sight depending on how familiar the reader is with the topics. Evidently, a lot of what is written predominantly affects the people of the world and it is time the people of the world stood up and reclaimed their world. I cannot stress this importance enough! The disclosure is also a basis which explains many of the anomalies which exist in the world today. I apologise in advance if the disclosure is too shocking to be believable (initially) and it shakes the foundations of your belief systems... but as I've said, rather than lash out at the information, you must question your own belief system... and probe into the mechanisms which have influenced you to adopt your current belief system... only then does the shock subside... and you can move forward with an open mind through investigation, which should lead you to either corroborate or debunk the disclosure. Keep in your heart: scepticism, optimism and open mindedness (Campbell 2008). Scepticism keeps you from believing fallacies. It keeps you from falling into that which you have not yet proven for yourself. Scepticism is a requirement for breakthroughs. Optimism gives you the ability to give merit to that which you have not yet proven for yourself and Open Mindedness gives you the ability to "see" that which has not yet been proven.

## *The Science of Hidden Consciousness*

Furthermore, "Consciousness Science Kept Hidden" (YesEthan 2013) illustrates:

- "The heart is an electrical organ. It produces by far the strongest form of bio electricity in our body; up to 40-60 times stronger than the second most powerful source –which is the brain. This electrical energy travels through every single cell in our body and in a sense, binds the cells together. The bio-electricity field is strong enough that it can even be detected outside of the body; out into space; beyond the skin. It is very measurable electromagnetic energy, much like radio waves. What we found is that the heart produces an electromagnetic field that surrounds our entire body 360 degrees; and it can be detected about 3-4 feet with megatron meters outside of the body. Researchers at the medical facility in Kansas, say they have detected it 10-12 feet. So regardless of how far it goes, what is interesting is that we produce this electromagnetic field which can be detected; it can be measured, with sensitive mainstream medical equipment." -Howard Martin (co Author) "The Heart Math Solution""
- Scientific studies have shown: that the heart is not only the most powerful centre in the body, it is the most intelligent and has the ability to receive precognition (knowledge of a future event or situation, especially outside one's normal sense of perception). If we can create coherence with our heart and mind centre we can access our intuition more frequently.

When you read my disclosure, remember that it is the heart and NOT the brain which is the most powerful centre in the body; the heart is the most intelligent; it has the ability to receive precognition and intuition about a future event, **before it actually occurs**; therefore if you find that your heart is in resonance with the themes I disclose; do not fight it with the ego of the mind; when our egos get in the way it overrides our heart's intuition; your heart is capable of discerning the truth of an event before your brain becomes conscious of it; by all means listen to your heart, and allow your brain to naturally develop its intuition. It will be the coherence between your heart first, and then your mind centre which will allow you to access your intuition.

Make an effort and reach your own conclusions to the point where you feel comfort in the fact that you **KNOW** the information contained in this disclosure is indeed factual. This will be the point you will have become empowered with golden truth and compelled to fulfil your duty as a human being and also spread the truth far and wide. Yes, we are all living in very interesting times.

## *Disclosure: Donald Marshall's Message to the World*

My name is Donald Marshall. I have been cloned by a large secretive cult know as "The Freemasons" and "The Vril Society" and "Scientologist" together called the Illuminati. For readers unfamiliar with The Illuminati, see "The New World Order" (1990) by A. Ralph Epperson and Appendix C in this document; an introductory guide to the Illuminati and their agenda for the world is presented.

Furthermore, I have to tell you that human cloning has been done since 1945. Now is also a very good time to recall Phil Schneider's comment (Schneider was a Geologist and Engineer who worked on black projects and Deep Underground Military Bases (DUMBs)): "That for every 12 months which passes, military technology advances by a rate of 44 years compared to the technology the public is currently accustomed to" (Schneider 1995; 1996; Open Minds 2011). George Green (a former Financier affiliated with U.S. Presidential candidates) also attests to the fact that humans have been cloned since 1938 (Project Camelot 2008a; 2008b). Therefore if we take 1945 as a base year, then military technology or hidden technology has advanced by the rate equivalent to 3080 years than the technology the general public is currently accustomed to (2015 – 1945 = 70 years; 70 multiplied by 44 = 3080). So yes, humans have been cloned since 1945 and continue to be cloned today and that current hidden technology in the year 2015 is as much as 3000 years ahead of the technology the public is currently accustomed to. I'll repeat myself because it is **very important** the reader understands the above statement, even if, the rest of the disclosure is hard to fathom after first read. The two **most important** things to keep in mind are:
1) Humans have been cloned for over 70 years (since 1945);
2) **Present** hidden technology is more advanced -as much as 3080 years more advanced -than what the public is currently accustomed to, and technology continues to advance at an incredible rate.

## *The Two Types of Cloning Techniques*

Now there are two different types of cloning techniques, there is replication cloning and duplication cloning. Replication cloning is the type of cloning the public has generally heard of. Replication cloning involves taking the nucleus (the DNA) out of a donor egg, and replacing it with new DNA from the person to be cloned. After a few days the resulting embryo can be implanted for pregnancy. The newborn starts life off as a genetic copy of an original.

Duplication cloning, on the other hand, is the second hidden method and type of cloning where the DNA from the person is grown in a big thick tank full of (salty) water. It involves a method of regenerative technology where the cells are agitated and agitated and over the course of 5 months, a fully formed duplicate clone body of an original is developed. The Illuminati used to have to use a tissue sample from the original or the cells from women's pap smears because this contained rich cells to make duplicate clones; they also used children's foreskins which were discarded at the hospital that got removed. That is what happened to me. I had my foreskin removed at age 4 –and by age 5 the Illuminati grew duplicate clones of me. Now the Illuminati say they have upgraded the technology since 2000 and now all they need is blood from the original. They then agitate the blood cells over and over again through regenerative technology, until a fully formed duplicate clone body of an original is produced. For readers who are unfamiliar with regenerative procedures, see Dr Stephen Badylak's video on "How to grow a new fingertip" (Science Channel 2014) and Carmichael (2013) which discuses how scientists cloned a mouse from a blood sample (this is another example of drip-feed disclosure). Regenerative science and medicine (CBS 2008) does work; I've seen it many times.

## *The Different Grades of Clones: "Mark 1" to "Mark 4" Clones*

There are a few different grades of clones that I know of. There are: "Mark 1" to "Mark 4" clones. Mark 1 clones were available at the end of World War II (1945). Mark 1 clones were rapid eye movement (REM) driven clones but they were primitive grades of clones with lots of side effects caused to the original.  Mark 1, REM driven clones were called "Organic Robotoids", even though there are no robotic parts to the clone at all. See Dr Peter Beter's discussion on "Organic Robotoids" (Beter 2011).

## *Donald Marshall's Dilemma with "Mark 2" Sleep Driven REM Clones*

The problem I am having is with Mark 2 REM driven clones. "Mark 2" is a rapid eye movement (REM) driven clone. In other words, Mark 2 clones are sleep driven clones. REM sleep is the fifth stage of sleep (Sleepdex 2015). The first REM cycle usually happens 90 minutes to 110 minutes **after** we fall asleep (Sleepdex 2015). What that means is: **currently,** this is the Illuminati's main form of communication. They do not call people on the phone; they do not meet at the Bohemian Grove anymore (they only meet there once a year for traditional purposes). Since they discovered the science of sleep driven cloning, they meet at the cloning centre **WHEN THEY GO TO SLEEP** (the cloning centre is a physical location, located 5 / 6 hours radius from the Robert Pickton Farm (Port Coquitlam, British Columbia, Canada) at a nature reserve).

## *Consciousness Transfer Happens When the Original Reaches REM Sleep*

The Illuminati can transfer the consciousness of an original once the person reaches REM sleep if there is a duplicate clone of the original at the cloning centre, once the person goes to sleep (90 minutes to 110 minutes after falling asleep). So what happens is that the consciousness of the original is transferred to the duplicated clone body (the duplicated clone body is grown within 5 months by regenerative technology) once the original reaches REM sleep. The original's consciousness is transferred from the original's body, although the original's body is still in their bed, asleep at home; to a duplicated REM driven clone body at the cloning centre and the original 'wakes up' as a cloned version of himself / herself at the cloning centre. It is a great marvel of science and one man's greatest achievements, but it is kept hidden and used for sinister purposes which I discuss below. I must address the readers at this point who are lost at the thought of duplication cloning, and consciousness transfer.

For readers who may have difficulty understanding the process of duplication cloning, see the video which features Dr Stephen Badylak (CBS 2008; Science Channel 2014). Badylak describes and illustrates how a new fingertip can be grown within 4 weeks, by the process of regenerative technology. Duplication cloning works a similar way; involving regenerative technology whereby the cells are agitated and agitated, and over the course of 5 months a fully formed duplicate clone body of an original is grown. Moreover, readers should also view the Horizon documentary "Why Do We Dream?" (2009); the documentary clearly explains the phases of sleep; particularly REM sleep. The documentary also clearly explains that during REM phase sleep the whole body shuts down, and it is only the brain which is active. The fact that the brain is still active, although the body is inactive, is a perfect opportunity for consciousness transfer; and this is usually the moment the Illuminati transfer the consciousness of a person who is asleep, to a cloned version of himself / herself. The reader should also explore Ehrsson's (2013) lecture on consciousness transfer. In the video, Ehrsson (2013) clearly explains how through the first person visual perspective (seeing through the eyes), and through synchronous (occurring at the same time) stimulation of a body part, individuals can perceive and see the world from another body different from their original. In other words, so long as people can see through the eyes, and the body is stimulated, the match between the visual perspective and feeling body sensations allows the individual to see and perceive the world through another body different from their original. The consciousness has been transferred to another body.

Ehrsson (2013) also demonstrates that consciousness is linked. Once consciousness is transferred (from the original's body to the new body), even though the new body is not the persons original body; when the new body is attacked, because the person perceives the world through the new body, everything feels "very real". When the new body (for which the person's consciousness has been transferred to) is attacked, the original still perceives the threat as "real", and therefore the person displays a biological and physiological fear response in their original body; the heart rate increases, as does respiration (breathing) rate, as well as anxiety.

### *Donald Marshall is an Original as he sits at Home Typing this Disclosure*

This is how advanced technology is today. This is also exactly what happens to me. **I am an original as I sit at home here typing this disclosure,** but when I enter REM sleep, my entire original body shuts down, and only my brain is active. The Illuminati have linked my consciousness to a REM driven duplicate clone body of me. Therefore, as soon as I enter REM sleep, they are alerted to the fact that I have entered stage five of the sleep cycle, and in REM sleep, because they have a green and red light above duplicate clones at the cloning centre. The red light indicates that the original is awake, and the green light lets them know that original has entered REM phase sleep and it is time to transfer their consciousness to a duplicate clone version. They cannot transfer the consciousness of an original before REM phase or when the original is awake. When they try and transfer consciousness before an original is in REM phase it makes the original have intense headaches. Setting an alarm every 90 minutes to wake up and then go back to sleep also does not work in terms of avoiding REM sleep and having your consciousness transferred, because the body requires REM sleep, and therefore you become very tired, quickly, if you do not get REM sleep. If you stay awake for four days without REM sleep you begin to hallucinate; after seven days without REM sleep you will die.

# When Donald Marshall's REM Driven Cloned Experiences Began

This whole sordid episode began when I was 5 years old, after going to the doctors to get my foreskin removed, at age 4. The tissues from my discarded foreskin were used to grow multiple duplicate clones of me. Within months, I was having my consciousness transferred to a REM driven, 5 year old clone version of me every time I entered REM sleep. The reason the Illuminati did this was because they wanted to use me as what they term "a diddle kid" – in other words they wanted to have sex with an REM driven, 5 year old, duplicate clone version of me. This is what they do. They clone people. They make duplicate clone bodies of people to victimise in terrible ways, and they clone children for men with undeveloped penises to have sex with.

However, I could never remember any of these REM driven clone experiences when I woke up for 25 years; because another aspect of REM driven cloning is that the Illuminati have the advantage of being able to suppress the experiences of people who have their consciousness transferred to their REM driven duplicate clone versions through advanced memory suppression technologies. For the reader who wishes to understand how memory suppression works see Winter (2014). Memories are stored and retrieved from different parts of the brain. Interactions between the cerebral cortex (the outer layer of the brain) and hippocampus need to work together in order to bring the memories out of mental storage to be re-experienced by the mind (Winter 2014). Therefore all that has to be done is for them to turn off the nerve cells which communicate with the cerebral cortex and hippocampus for the evening which you went to sleep and had your consciousness transferred to a REM driven duplicate clone version of you, and you will not remember anything. The technology is so advanced; they can, and do suppress memories at a push of a button. Therefore, the victim wakes up the next morning and will not remember a single REM driven duplicate clone experience. All that they will be aware of is that they did not have a dream the previous night.

This is what happened to me for over 25 years. I wasn't allowed to remember these REM driven duplicate clone experiences until I turned 30. My memories were suppressed for 25 years. I would wake up many days, after a night's sleep, thinking 'I didn't have a dream last night'; or I would wake up the next morning and I would be sick, although I went to sleep the previous night feeling completely healthy. Throughout the years, I thought I had terminal illness; because whenever I went to see a doctor, the diagnosis would always come back that 'there was nothing wrong with me'.

However, over the course of 25 years when I was memory suppressed, and not allowed to remember my REM sleep driven clone experiences, the Illuminati were using me to produce songs, lots and lots of songs, and whenever I could not produce a song, or did not want to, they would stab my REM driven clone body; sodomize my REM driven clone body; chain me to a crucifix and burn my REM driven clone and torture me for all kinds different reasons; and even when I was compliant and did what they told me to, I was attacked, simply because some members of the Illuminati wanted to know what it feels like to stab someone. Now because consciousness is linked (Ehrsson 2013), all these REM clone torture experiences affected me in my original body, and I have a weak heart today because of it, at the age of 39. The memories of my REM clone driven experiences also had to be released to me slowly (see Alford (2014) and FW: Thinking (2014) –for an example of how memories can be wiped and restored) over the course of many months because I had been through so much horror and torture that if the memories was released all at once, I would have had a heart attack in my real body and died.

This is one of the main reasons the Illuminati currently use REM sleep driven cloning (besides sex and torture): to plagiarise talented people under duress. There are many people including me who have been, and are plagiarised on a daily basis. Their consciousness is transferred to their REM driven clone alternates, and night after night and under duress they are forced to reveal their money making ideas or face torture or clone death; clone death after clone death. That is what the movie *Inception* (2010) is about: REM sleep driven cloning, and stealing ideas from the minds of unsuspecting individuals. The Illuminati actually made the film *Inception* (2010) as well as *The Island* (2005), *Avatar* (2009) and *The 6th Day* (2000); the films mentioned above contain references of cloning and REM driven cloning to show off the Illuminati's 'power' and throw in the world's face and laugh.

## *The Science of REM Driven Cloning Began in 1945*

I am one of the few people fortunate, or unfortunate depending on how you look at it, who remembers all of my REM driven cloning experiences because these memories were released to me at the age of 30. I remember many people who have attended and still attend the cloning centre which they bring me to over the course of 34 years. I am currently 39 years old and was brought there since the age of 5. The science of REM sleep driven cloning was first discovered in 1945, and at first it was just a political thing which leaders of the world did. Through the science of REM sleep driven cloning, political figures, heads of state and royalty met each other as REM driven clones versions of their selves when they went to sleep and discussed worldly affairs in complete secret with each other. They also did whatever they wanted with each other as REM driven clones, which they could not do in their original bodies; such as sex, fighting each other to the death, jumping off cliffs as their REM driven clones, and just about anything you can think of when one has the ability of pseudo-immortality as a sleep driven clone version of themselves hidden from the guise of the world and general public.

Well they soon got bored of each other very quickly, and started to make REM driven duplicate clones of movie stars, musicians, celebrities and public figures from all walks of life to hang with as REM driven clones and now they all get together for a disgusting time as REM driven clones when they go to sleep. Most of the G20 political leaders meet at the cloning centre as REM driven clones when they go to sleep to discuss worldly matters and watch gruesome things done to innocent and unsuspecting civilians, who are also REM sleep driven clones at the cloning centre, but civilians have their memories suppressed. This is what the films *Hostel* (2006); *Hostel: Part II* (2007); and *Hostel: Part III* (2011) (Illuminati made films) -are about: -rich people paying to torture and kill innocent people at a secluded location for sport; just that at the cloning centre, the Illuminati members torture and kill REM driven clones of innocent people.

Therefore, depending on what was done to your REM driven clone, you could wake up the next day with a very intense headache in your **original body**, if your REM clone was repeatedly punched in the head; an upset stomach in your **original body** if your internal organs were tortured; achy limbs; and worst of all, feel sick all over; although the previous evening you went to sleep feeling healthy. Remember consciousness is linked (Ehrsson 2013), therefore whatever happens to your REM driven clone will affect you in your original body. Even when they suppress your memory; the previous night's experiences still affects you in your original body. You wake up with the knowledge that you did not dream the previous evening when you went to sleep, and with certain illnesses depending on what was done to your REM driven clone.

## _Help Donald Marshall STOP REM Driven Cloning NOW!_

Everything I discuss in this disclosure is firsthand witness accounts. I have seen and experienced horror spectacles done to innocent civilians and to me. For the sake of humanity and the innocent children brought to the cloning centres all over the world; I must tell the whole world about this and the good people of this world **MUST HELP ME TO BRING THIS TO A STOP.** My sense of duty, moral correctness, and conscience cannot allow me to stay silent about this evil. REM sleep driven cloning, and the torture of innocent civilians as REM driven clones; having REM driven clone sex with beautiful, innocent unsuspecting civilians of the world; the paedophilia of children through the process of REM driven cloning; REM driven sex slavery; the plagiarism of talented individuals through the process of REM driven cloning; and REM driven idea slavery, whereby talented individuals must produce new ideas and concepts daily (or whenever they sleep) or be stabbed or tortured in their sleep as REM clones –is the most vicious and pernicious form of tyranny ever to occur against humanity and **IT MUST BE STOPPED NOW!**

## _Do Not Panic, Riot, or Cause Chaos. This is Very Important._

Now I must preface this carefully, because members of the Illuminati have told me that I have to put this in an eloquent fashion, in a way which does not make people panic because people finding out about REM driven cloning, and the extent of the evil it has been used for, and continues to be used for; it could cause loss of social order, riots and anarchy in the streets. Moreover, I too **DO NOT** want riots and anarchy in the streets, despite the fact that I am vehemently angry considering the extent to which they plagiarised my talents over the years. If you are a good person reading this, and you want to help and you want social order restored for the benefit of mankind, promise yourself; me; all the innocent children they have affected through REM driven cloning, and the children of the future that you will **NOT** riot, and destroy a world for children who are going to inherit the world. **This is very important**. Remember the Illuminati have highly advanced technologies (kept hidden and secret), including weaponry, and they are just waiting for any excuse to use it on the populace. In all revolutions, the populace always win, and I want this disclosure and the end of REM driven sleep cloning to go smoothly. I want the good people of the world to keep spreading this information, keep spreading this disclosure all over social media, tell your close friends, your family, and as many people on social media platforms as you can. The internet, and radio shows with small audiences are the only forms of communication the Illuminati do not control. They own all forms of television networks, even including the Aboriginal People's Television Network (APTN), and therefore a message as important as this will never reach the average man or woman through television because it does not serve their agenda.

## _Spread this Disclosure Document until it reaches the Armed Forces_

I want this message to reach the armed forces, because currently people in the armed forces are following orders, yet they do not know how corrupt their governments and people in high profile places are. They are unknowingly defending these corrupt people. People in the armed forces will **NOT** defend these corrupt people nor will they harm civilians when they realise that these corrupt people have been growing duplicate clone bodies of civilians, transferring civilians consciousness to their duplicate clone versions when the victim reaches REM sleep, and torturing civilians in their sleep; having sex with under-aged REM driven cloned children; having sex with innocent and unsuspecting adults as REM driven sleep clones, against their will; torturing REM driven clones for sport; and for money-making ideas to benefit their own pockets while they make innocent civilians sick and have side effects in their original bodies from REM sleep driven cloning technology. No. The armed forces will not accept that. Therefore keep spreading and sharing this information for everyone to see so that it reaches personnel in the armed forces **ASAP!** I want the armed forces to overthrow these corrupt people. The Illuminati think they are very sly and untouchable because together they hold most of the wealth in the world. We must show them that they are not untouchable. Please do all you can, to share and spread this message. It is the most important message to ever reach the internet because it affects all our liberties.

I must also address the readers who may feel afraid in spreading my message because they may want to do the right thing, but they are terrified the Illuminati may degrade or end their lives. As unbelievable as the next thing I am going to share sounds, it is a belief system which shapes the reality of the Illuminati and therefore they themselves are afraid to do anything which may degrade their lives or 'eternal soul'.

They believe that they are the 'fornicators' mentioned in The Bible, and if they were to degrade or harm the lives of anyone aiding me, they would suffer the wrath of God when they die. Notice I said **when they die**, but so long as they are still alive they can do all the evil they like, with little consequence, as they do in their REM driven clone versions at the cloning centre; worshipping Lucifer and doing all sorts of ungodly things. They even say God does not exist, only science and technology; yet they are afraid of dying. Very afraid of dying; because they believe they'll meet God's judgement. I'm just relaying what they have told me. They are weird like that. They also follow Hopi Indian Prophecy, Mayan Prophecy and Nostradamus Prophecy. They mix and match those three prophecies and come up with their own religion of what may or may not happen in the future.

## Donald Marshall is NOT "The New Age Saviour". Nobody wants to be a 'saviour'

Furthermore, **THEY** believe I am a new age saviour for the end times; that I was going to save the world from something, according to the Nostradamus prophecy (quatrains); the Illuminati consider Nostradamus the greatest prophet ever to walk the earth. They are in awe of him.

I **DO NOT** endorse their claims. I just want REM driven cloning to stop and these people face punishments for their crimes against humanity. I really do not endorse such claims, but if it saves my life and yours, so be it. In reality and practicality, nobody wants to be 'the saviour'; not with such tyranny and pernicious evil such as this. We'd rather all just be living normal lives without the knowledge and practice of REM driven sleep cloning which is used for torture, clone death spectacles and sex with children. My friends on Facebook do not want to be heroes or 'saviours' either; nobody really does, but we do it out of a sense of duty, moral correctness and our conscience would never rest knowing the true extent of evil in this world, and doing nothing to end it. So all that saviour and Nostradamus prophecy talk, it is just the Illuminati; they like to quote prophecies, and make them come true to make themselves feel special.

Like I said, they are weird. I'm just relaying what they say, and I **do not** endorse the new age saviour claims. I'm just a normal guy, who was unfortunate to be cloned when he had his foreskin removed at age 4. This could have happened to anyone. Thankfully I had a very active imagination at the age of 5 and with the use of the technologies such as Mind-voice technology (that is what the Illuminati call it) it allowed me to make songs to keep the perverts off me. Mind-voice technology is just a technology which can tune into the inner voice in your head (See articles by Prigg (2014) and New Scientist (2014) –which discuss how scientist can listen to your inner voice; –it is similar to how Mind-voice technology works). Therefore, when you hear the sound of a guitar; the sound of drums; or any instrument for that matter; after hearing the sound, when you imagine the sound you heard, your REM driven clone can replicate this sound with Mind-voice technology **exactly**; and I used Mind-voice technology to make many, many, songs over the years. As I've said, and I'll say it again: technology today is very advanced.

## *How the Nostradamus Prophecies shapes the lives of the Illuminati*

Also another reason they have not killed me is because the Illuminati said "If they do, everyone is going to know I am telling the truth", -which I am with my right hand to God and I cannot lie about this stuff; the things I have seen are too sinister and diabolical. It would make me as bad as them if I did. Furthermore, because they follow the Nostradamus prophecies religiously, they have told me that they believe anyone helping me is considered part of "The Army of Light" and again, to hurt or degrade anyone helping me, considered part of The Army of Light would incur the wrath of God; and that to hurt anyone considered part of The Army of Light will degrade their lives; they will suffer misfortune and entire ruin as will their eternal soul. These are just some of the interpretations of the Nostradamus quatrains they have relayed to me. These people are beyond crazy, zealot and religious fanatics. Nevertheless, the main point to remember by all this is that **you are safe**, and **they cannot hurt you**, **they are scared to hurt you**, as well as kill me because prophecies have shaped their lives and the lives of their ancestors for hundreds of years.

Furthermore, and practically, I have told too many people that this is the extent, to which technology has developed in our current day, and it is kept secret and hidden from the public for nefarious purposes and this is what the Illuminati do: REM sleep driven cloning. I have been spreading this information **since 2011** and not one of these high profile people, government officials or celebrity figures has issued a (public) statement against me or taken me to court over libel charges because I'm telling the truth; and their statements would not hold in court.

I have also told over a million Arabs; I have appeared on radio interviews with Vinny Eastwood (Vincent Eastwood 2013); Jeanice Barcelo (Jeanice Barcelo 2013); and Lisa Phillips on the Cry Freedom Radio show (Astral 7ight 2013a – 2013h). I have reached audiences as many as 280,000 views on the Vinny Eastwood Show (Vincent Eastwood 2013) alone. However, I must stress that YouTube reduces the view count of my interviews every so often in order to suppress the truth so that my interviews do not get featured on their platform. Nevertheless, there is safety in numbers and rest assured there are new people waking up to the disclosure of REM driven sleep cloning every day; and therefore you can share and spread this information **without any worry** about facing reprisals from the Illuminati, even if you do not believe that it is in fact their beliefs in Nostradamus prophecies which is saving you and I from the Illuminati.

## *HIV/AIDS has been cured; so have many forms of cancer*

Now is also a good time to share with the reader that this situation is not all 'doom and gloom'. In their quest to perfect technologies, science and medicine, the Illuminati discovered the cure for HIV/AIDS; cancer (except pancreatic cancer); Alzheimer's; Dementia, and many more debilitating diseases which humanity suffers with. They relayed the fact that they found the cure for HIV/AIDS by stimulating the cells in an oxygenated rich environment because diseases/viruses cannot thrive in an oxygenated rich environment (in layman's terms). Magic Johnson was cured from AIDS this way and they use him as a spokesperson to sell the retrovirus pills which they know is not as effective. However, the greed these people have, knows no bounds, and because they receive too many donations for HIV/AIDS as well as cancer donations they do not announce they have cured HIV/AIDS or cancer publicly. As I've told you, and will continue to tell you: technology is far, far, FAR advanced than what you currently see around you. With the help of the good people of earth I promise to release these technologies for the benefit of mankind, and all reading this disclosure can hold me to this. You **must** hold me to this. It is time we ended corrupt governments and corrupt individuals in high positions of power in this world. Hold me to this.

I hope you are now beginning to understand why this is a **world emergency** and why these corrupt people must be ousted and overthrown. I also hope you understand why you must not riot or cause chaos because as I said at the beginning of this disclosure "I write this to empower good people of the world against the tyranny which exists all around us in our world today"; I **did NOT** write this to cause chaos, public dissension or anarchy. Good people of the world will inherit the earth once these corrupt people are overthrown. Therefore, under no circumstance must you destroy the world when you are going to inherit it. No matter how angry this disclosure makes you; no matter how angry the diabolical people who commit these crimes against humanity make you feel. Let's make sure this goes smoothly. Keep spreading and sharing this information, until this disclosure reaches the armed forces; until the armed forces bring these corrupt people to their knees. We are about to inherit the earth; by all means let's ensure everything goes smoothly. Now that you understand how important this disclosure is and that the overthrow of these corrupt individuals must progress smoothly, I'll continue.

## *The Behaviour of High Profile People at the Cloning Centre*

The high profile individuals who attend these REM driven clone gatherings in their sleep have nothing better to do than to show off in disgusting ways. They have no shame and it seems nothing embarrasses them. Some REM sleep driven, cloning centre attendees, sit in the stands of an unused arena, smaller than a hockey rink, but it still has the capacity to seat between approximately 300 to 400 people. There is dirt in the centre of the rink where ice would be. They have frightened REM driven clones of children walk into the middle of the dirt rink to be victimised for a bizarre and disgusting spectacle. Sometimes, they have animals like dogs have sex with the REM driven clone children, while a man holds the dogs on leash so that it wouldn't bite the child on the back of the neck; which I have seen happen before. They all try to outdo each other in their levels of depravity; to be evil is to be "cool" to them.

## *The Ring Leaders of the Cloning Centre*

I will now discuss the ring leaders, but before I name names, please understand that I am not someone who has collated stories and evidence together over the internet. I REALLY **do not** need to do this. Every time I enter REM sleep, the ring leaders at the cloning centre transfer my consciousness to a duplicate clone version of me. I have seen and talked with these monsters over the course of 34 years as REM driven clones at the cloning centre. However, I do understand that for the average reader, without understanding how far medicine, science and technology has advanced; without seeing or hearing people, other than me, discuss the crimes the ring leaders of the cloning centres commit, it is very difficult to imagine that this is what these high profile people are involved with, and do. Nevertheless, I guarantee it; this is the true extent and prevalence of evil in our world.

Their public personas, and public images is well managed by their PR teams, and therefore for the average person it is difficult to imagine these people in any other way but "positive"; but these people behind closed doors are the most evil, sick and twisted people I have ever had the misfortune of encountering. It is also difficult to take in what I am saying because I am not a public figure, nor do I have the "influence" or public image these people have; the general populace have never met, or heard of me, or known who I am; if this was the case my eye witness testimony alone will be enough; however, I do understand that we are dealing with highly advanced technologies, thousands of years advanced compared to what the general public is accustomed to, and because of this I provide references for the reader; I provide references for the reader to have something to corroborate what I am disclosing; and I provide references for the reader to see pass the illusions these people have created.

Moreover, as "Consciousness Science Kept Hidden" demonstrates (YesEthan 2013): remember that it is the heart and not the brain which is the most powerful centre in the body, the heart is the most intelligent; it has the ability to receive precognition and intuition about a future event, **before it actually occurs**, therefore if you find that your heart is in resonance with the names mentioned; do not fight it with the ego of the mind; when our egos get in the way it overrides our heart's intuition; your heart is capable of discerning the truth of an event before your brain becomes conscious of it; by all means listen to your heart, and allow your brain to naturally develop its intuition. It will be the coherence between your heart first, and then your mind centre which will allow you to access your intuition.

The references I provide for the reader to corroborate what I am about to say includes: "Appeal from Survivors of Canadian Genocide" (inifiniLor 2013); Tila Tequila –"Missing Children and Cloning Centres" (Astral 7ight 2013i); "Royal Babylon by Heathcote Williams" (MrCowshedder 2012); and "THIS MOVIE WILL BLOW YOUR F%SNG MIND" (KafkaWinstonWorld 2014).

Watch all the above videos and you will easily see all that I disclose. In Appeal from Survivors of Canadian Genocide interview (inifiniLor 2013): Listen to the indigenous people Stee-mas and Wahtsek speak about the pain and torment they have suffered under the Crown, the Vatican, the government, and churches of Canada. 50,000 to 150,000 indigenous children have gone missing because of the involvement of the Crown, the Vatican, the government, and the churches of Canada; and all these factions involved know this!

Tila Tequila is a television personality who has attended the cloning centres as a REM driven clone since childhood. In Tila Tequila's radio phone in (Astral 7ight 2013i), the audio is not very clear for the majority of her disclosure; she was also frightened and therefore she sounds most animated; however her words are clear at the following points of the audio (I also provide a transcript in the appendices section: "Appendix A"):

4.00 min: Cloning Centres and they take your children...
4.25 min: –There are these CLONING CENTRES –I'm not even talking about child molestation here...
5.40 min –They take your children –they not only molest them; men f*** them; and make them shoot each other...
7.59 min- There is a point where you cannot just turn the other way, you know this stuff is going on and you go 'oh well, you know... that's their problem; let's just turn the other cheek. How long are you going to turn the other cheek until it happens to your own freaking children?

10.34 min - Do you know why they love children? Because they are innocent souls; they are innocent... they are the most innocent, pure beings in this planet. They are not harmed by anything. They are new to the world; bright-eyed, pure innocent children. That is why these disgusting paedophile... and these clone rings, cloning centres, satanic rituals, Brownsville Texas... there are many of the of the cloning centres where they take your children that go missing.

Royal Babylon by Heathcote Williams (MrCowshedder 2012) addresses the fact that for Brits, despite their inordinate pride about their tradition, it is often revealed they know little about it than anyone. The documentary then goes on to address the fact that Prince Phillip the Duke of Edinburgh, has a lust for blood-sports which includes shooting endangered wildlife and mammals which he considers 'culling'. The documentary is also notable for demonstrating to the viewer that Queen Elizabeth II redistributed as much as 2.1 million for her private income from 276 people from Merseyside and Lancashire. These people had no will, so their property was grabbed. The same is true for the Duchy of Cornwall. If you die without making a will, everything you possess will go to Prince Charles. Furthermore, Queen Elizabeth II is the largest land owner on earth. Queen Elizabeth II: head of state of the United Kingdom, and 31 other states and territories is the legal owner of about 6600 million acres of land; one six of the earth's non ocean surface. She is the only person on earth who owns whole countries, and who owns countries that are not her own domestic territory. This land ownership is separate from her role as head of state; is different from other monarchies where no such claim is made –Norway, Belgium, Denmark etc. The value of her land holding is £17,600,000,000,000 (17.6 trillion Pounds) (approximately)).

In "THIS MOVIE WILL BLOW YOUR F%SNG MIND" (KafkaWinstonWorld 2014), readers with a deeper knowledge of the Illuminati and the agenda of the Illuminati will easily spot the minor inaccuracies in the documentary. However, the documentary provides a good reference and foundation for anyone new to the topic of the Illuminati and their agendas for the world. The documentary demonstrates how the world is currently a deception within a deception coated in reverse psychology. It gives widespread insight into the Royal family of England, and their lineage.

Furthermore, the documentary provides information that the world's most popular religions have been infiltrated with Illuminati dogma, in secret. The documentary details how (some) modern Christians, Jews, and Muslims do not (yet) recognise their common enemy because that enemy is invisible (until now). The enemy hides within their own religions. The enemy also hides within the activist community (anti-Illuminati movements), it finances big budget documentaries and movements. The end game is to sell a divisive (creating strong disagreement), anti-capitalistic, atheistic message and deliver trusting followers right into the lap of a communist (one government) New World Order. The enemy is the Illuminati.

The documentary also details that: "Today, the bloodlines of this unholy alliance are on the final stages of establishing one world religion, one world government, and one world ruler [-- that is IF, the good people of this world do nothing to stop them]. The Windsor Royals are at the control of this web of deceit. It is a known fact that Adam Weishaupt (the founder of the Illuminati) took refuge and got assistance from the German Saxe-Coburg Gotha Royal family. The Saxe-Coburg Gotha's changed their German name to Windsor (in 1917). The Windsor's public image is a façade, to hide the cesspool from which they operate behind the scenes; their power and control cascades out of Buckingham Palace to the elite bloodlines who run world affairs."

For anyone who thinks they know they Royal family of England, did you know that still to this day: they have a person appointed called "Groom of the Stool"? What is a "Groom of the stool", you may ask? A Groom of the stool is responsible for stools. The kind you sit on and the kind you expel. In other words a Groom of the Stool wipes Royal bottoms. The above has been confirmed to me by Prince Charles of Wales himself as REM driven clones at the cloning centre, and I quote: "It gives you the feeling of being completely taken care of" when I asked Prince Charles (as a REM driven clone) why they still have that. But don't just take my word for this; research "Groom of the Stool".

## *The Royal Family of England*

As most of readers have already guessed; and as unbelievable as it may currently sound to some readers, the ring leaders of these cloning centres includes the royal family of England. As I've said REM driven cloning started as far back as 1945, and it was just a political thing, but Queen Elizabeth II has been involved with REM driven cloning since its inception! Yes! Queen Elizabeth II; Phillip, Duke of Edinburgh and Prince Charles of Wales are the worst of them. They are unbelievable depraved perverts all showing off to the celebrities who attend these REM driven clone gatherings. Elizabeth has the REM sleep driven cloned children at the cloning centre call her "Lilli-bet" and Elizabeth as a REM driven clone herself does ungodly things to these REM driven cloned children. Some she fakes being nice to; some she is terrible to; and as a REM sleep driven clone Elizabeth cuts these REM driven clone children with swords while they scream. The decent people at these cloning centres who have had their consciousness transferred into their duplicate REM driven clones, and are there against their will, like I am; they are terrified to say anything against Elizabeth and her cronies. Most of these decent people also have their children's consciousness transferred into their REM driven duplicate clones, and Elizabeth and her cronies hold these decent peoples' children as hostage; to be torn apart; clone death after clone death if they have the slightest inkling of informing anyone, but as Elizabeth and her cohort have been torturing me as REM driven sleep clones anyway, I will disclose all that they do.

Vladimir Putin is also there, as an REM driven clone, and he loves to put the fear of torture and death into people, but he is essentially a perverted coward himself. Most of the famous people who attended the cloning centre as REM driven clones are ashamed to speak or be seen by me there very much; because they are ashamed of the perverse and disgusting gatherings. I am a decent person, even when my consciousness is transferred to my REM duplicate clone alternative, and I will not participate in these depraved acts; so they use me as an example and torture me for being a good person. They have drugged my REM driven clone, and as I've mentioned because consciousness transfer is real (Ehrsson 2013) and because consciousness is linked, therefore everything feels "real as real"; when I'm drugged as a REM driven clone, I behave exactly as any person would on hard drugs (although I have never taken any drugs in my original body); my vision is blurry and my balance affected; they have used this as method of having me do disgusting things in a blurred state, videotaping these dirty acts and editing a highlight reel which also depicts me doing disgusting things to show to the world when the world learns of their depraved natures and their public personas are shattered so that I can be despised as much as they will be when the entire world learns about this. Furthermore, because of the microchip inserted in my REM driven clone; they mind controlled me like a "Manchurian Candidate" (*The Manchurian Candidate* 2004) using MK Ultra technology, which is far more advanced than the declassified MK Ultra techniques (MK Ultra Compendium 1980) mentioned online today which references MK Ultra techniques in the 1970s. See Rense (2001) for a detailed explanation of how implanted microchips work, and how these chips allow the programmer control victims. C.S.I.S Canadian intelligence are all involved; they have REM driven clones too; including a lot of Commissionaires and Canadian Prime Minister Steven Harper himself; they do what Elizabeth says, and seem to follow her every whim without question. It doesn't matter who you are; if you have a cute child, or a talented child with imagination, creativity and moneymaking potential (such as business smarts; song making ability; literary / oratory ability etc. –you name it so long as your child has moneymaking value to them) they will send for the blood record of your child; agitate the blood cells over and over until a duplicate clone of your child is grown; they will then transfer your child's duplicate clone body from the tank they were grown onto a steel rack; the steel racks contain 5 rows and each row holds a duplicate cloned body; once your child goes to sleep in his or her original body and once they enter REM sleep (90 minutes to 110 minutes after they first fall asleep) the Illuminati are alerted to this fact by a green light above your child's duplicate clone at the cloning centre, and they then transfer your child's consciousness to the REM driven duplicate clone; this is the point where the prime evils molest your children; and so your children are being molested in their sleep as REM driven clones and then they suppress the child's memory or implant false memories (see Kim (2013) and Alford (2015) –on how false memories can be implanted) so your children wake up not remembering dreams from the previous night, or if they do remember anything, the memory is false. These depraved acts very much stunt children's development; it causes them to have learning disabilities; unexplained depression; loneliness; suicidal thoughts, and all kinds of side effects.

The cloning centre is a paedophiles paradise and **it must be stopped**! Elizabeth secretly owns a few music companies too (Universal and others) with bands under contract; she forces me under a knife to compose music for them; if I can't she will stab my REM driven clone; burn my REM driven clone and have her pervert thugs smash my REM driven clone body there. As Ehrsson (2013) demonstrated, because consciousness is linked; and consciousness transfer leads the person who has had their consciousness transferred to still perceive reality as "real as real" in the new body; I have the same biological and physiological responses as I would have if these attacks were occurring to my original body. This has caused me to have heart damage and severe debilitating headaches. Because my memories were released to me; I can now also remember all my past REM driven clone memories since age 5; as well as the previous night's REM driven cloned memories (when I have my consciousness transferred to the cloning centre) which causes severe stress to my mental psyche and mental well being.

As unbelievable as the above statement sounds regarding Elizabeth's ownership of music companies, just go and listen to the song "Abadon" performed by Boondox (RainmanJhof 2011) on YouTube. There are two "Abadon" versions; the version you seek can be found in the Reference section uploaded by RainmanJhof (2011); skip to 2:46 min (or listen to the whole song; pay particular attention at 2:46 min) and you will hear loud and clearly, Elizabeth say "Drop the mother f****ing base". That is Elizabeth's voice; you can compare it to any of her Christmas speeches. That is her. Elizabeth said the above as a REM driven clone at the cloning centre. I know. I was there. They got so confident, that nobody would ever find out about their REM driven cloning shenanigans, that they even had me sing on a song I produced: "Where'd You Go" –Fort Minor (Murdok Dubstep Remix) (MurdokDubstep 2010), available on YouTube. Tila Tequila and I sing on this remixed track as REM driven clones (MurdokDubstep 2010); I start to sing from 1:44 min onwards. You can compare the voice you hear in the song with the Vinny Eastwood interview (Vincent Eastwood 2013). That is me, in both cases, and that song was recorded at the cloning centre.

One good person at the cloning centre; Bernie Mac (also as an REM clone version of himself); who was an actor and comedian, tried to stand up for me and speak up for me, saying 'Cloning and torturing people here, it's not right to do to a human being...' and "This place is the devil'"... Bernie Mac also tried to have others join him in speaking out against the REM driven clone torture zone while he was having his consciousness transferred to his REM clone driven version. Elizabeth and Philip tortured him for 4 to 5 hours continuously at the cloning centre as an example of their 'power', Bernie Mac had an aneurysm (brain bleed) the next day and died. This is one of the aspects about REM driven clone torture: if you torture a REM driven clone continuously for hours on end, you will cause the person to die in their original body from a heart attack or aneurysm (while they sleep); even if they do manage to wake up the next day, because of the constant pain their consciousness has recorded and because consciousness is linked they will wake up only to have a heart attack or aneurysm in their original bodies the following day. If you apply a constant electrical current to a REM driven clone, that person will either have a heart attack or die from aneurysm in their original bodies while they sleep.

This form of murder is similar to the CIA's heart attack gun (Non Mirage Truth Vision 2015); which was declassified in the 1970s and was a weapon used for causing heart attacks in victims, undetectable as the cause of heart attack under autopsy. The difference with REM driven clone death as a form of weaponry is that hardly anyone has heard of death by REM driven clone torture. Moreover, the perpetrator can be thousands of miles away from the victim; the culprit just needs a duplicate REM driven clone of the victim to torture or apply a constant electrical current to; this is exactly what is going on in our world every day. When Elizabeth and Philip don't like someone and they want to get rid of that person, they clone that person; torture his or her REM driven clone until that person has a heart attack or aneurysm in their original body and dies.

This is what Elizabeth and Duke Phillip did to the indigenous people in Canada. The video reference (inifiniLor 2013) provided above, regarding the genocide of the indigenous people of Canada discusses this very topic (inifiniLor 2013). As Elizabeth and Duke Phillip visited Canada as clones, when they killed the native children; they both had solid alibis of being in England at the time. They then cloned all the witnesses of the Canadian missing children's case and had them remotely killed by applying constant electric currents to their REM driven clones; one by one and each witness either died of a heart attack or aneurysm. They just dispatched the last witness by also applying a constant electric current to the persons REM driven clone because the missing children's case was building momentum.

After Bernie Mac's death everyone is afraid to speak up; they all became afraid of suffering the same fate. All it will take is a few lie detector tests from an independent source; and I will volunteer for them; they cover up for themselves so carefully that lie detector tests from an independent source unconnected to them in anyway will be the only viable method. I know many non-famous people who have also attended these clone centre gatherings as their REM driven clone duplicate versions and also remember the clone gathering experiences in their original bodies (because they were not memory suppressed) that could be given lie detector tests to prove this. When it comes to the sexual exploitation of a child, lie detectors are admissible in Canadian courts. I need decent people with integrity to speak about this filthy business; to testify about who is involved. There is much to tell about the Illuminati and I am a wealth of information about this topic.

Elizabeth also had Princess Dianna Spencer killed by having someone shine the brightest light known to mankind through the window side on her car; they swerved away to avoid the light and hit the divider; it was no paparazzi. I first wrote about this in my original disclosure in **2011**; this was corroborated by an article 2 years **AFTER** I had made my original disclosure. See Radar Online (2013) for the corroborating article. Furthermore, "Candle in the wind" performed by Elton John (SadSongs4You 2010) was not Dianna's 'death song'; it was "Bigger than us" performed by "White Lies" (WhiteLiesVevo 2010). The Illuminati released this song, deliberately, 13 years after Dianna's death, again as a show of their 'power'. I did not want to compose this song but Elizabeth and her thugs threatened to stab and burn my REM driven clone repeatedly if I did not. Listen to the lyrics. I'll provide some of the lyrics here for those of you who are feeling too shocked by these revelations:

White Lies Lyrics "Bigger than us"

You took the tunnel route home.
You've never taken that way with me before.
Did you feel a need for change?
Apologies on your fingernails,
Love flickered in the city of lights
Like internet and radio waves.

I don't need your tears
I don't want your love
I've just got to get home

And I feel like I'm breaking up
But I wanted to stay.
Headlights on the hillside
Don't take me this way.
I don't want you to hold me
I want you to pray,
'cause it's bigger than us.

Are you beginning to see why these people must be stopped and stopped immediately? Are you beginning to see why it is no longer okay to 'turn a blind eye' or 'bury your head in the sand', and hope it all goes away? Can you see why I need the good people of this world to keep sharing this disclosure (online); to tell your friends and family until this information reaches the armed forces so that the armed forces can bring these people to their knees. I also do not want innocent civilians to get hurt despite the monstrosities these people cause to humanity on a daily basis. I want the overthrow to progress smoothly so that the good people of the earth can inherit the world, with all technologies and medical advancements which benefit mankind, made available to all. This is why I maintain my composure and resolve, in spite of the evil I see on a daily basis, and you the reader must also maintain your composure and resolve in spite of the evil which I am disclosing, so that we do not inherit a torn down world after we have completely overthrown these malevolent, sinister and corrupt hypocrites!

Furthermore, Diana survived the car crash; and while, either on her way to hospital or in hospital, Dianna was injected with a high concentration of salt, which is near undetectable in an autopsy and she died. Elizabeth did this because Diana was going to marry an Arab named Dodi Fayed. The Illuminati hate Arabs because for the most part, Arabs have not broken their relationship with God. Dianna hated her association with these people; Dianna knew about REM driven, sleep cloning and wanted nothing to do with it; but she was afraid of being killed and so said nothing. I know a lot about this and many more deplorable things the Illuminati have done over the course of 34 years and I will be more than happy to reveal all the evil they have done; as well as all the wonderful discoveries and progresses they have made in medicine, science and technology, which they have withheld from the general public. I am very happy to disclose all, because I know once the world learns of all they have done, we truly will begin to see the end of such evil on this planet. Just make sure you keep spreading this disclosure and it reaches the armed forces soon. Soon, soon, soon!

## _Help Donald Marshall by Sharing this Disclosure with Your Close Friends and Family_

If you are reading this, then you have to help me. I know some of you may be reading this thinking, but I am just an ordinary man or woman Donald, I know you are telling the truth; I can feel it in my heart and my head that what you say is true and that you are telling the truth (which I promise you, with my right hand to God I am) but I'm just an ordinary man / woman Donald; I don't have any power; I don't have any influence; or because of the position I am currently in I can't speak out against these people; and I am just an ordinary man / woman I cannot be expected to take on the world's problems. You are right if you are thinking and feeling this, and I do not expect or want you to take on the world's problems. All I want you to do is share this information with close friends and family initially, because when you do that, at least that is one more person who will know about the true extent of evil in this world. When your close friend or family member also shares my disclosure with another close friend, the disclosure will eventually spread exponentially. It will also be one more person who has your well being in their thoughts because I understand how scary it is to know this. Therefore remember **there is safety in numbers;** and the more people you tell in your social circle, the more you can all look out for each other. So feel free to share my disclosure with close friends and family. Do not talk about my disclosure in public (for now) if it makes you feel uncomfortable. Moreover, if you want to reach more people (other than your initial social circle) the best way, is to do it online: through social media, such as Facebook, Twitter, and YouTube etc. As I've already mentioned, the Illuminati controls all forms of media except the internet.

The Illuminati, being so 'confident' at the time with the evil they wield onto the world, put my face on a Megadeth album cover titled _The World Needs a Hero_ (2001) (to mock me) when I was 23. I posed for this album cover at the cloning centre when I was 23, and the album was released with a picture of my face, as a REM driven clone, 3 years later when I was 26. They did this because they were extremely confident that nothing would ever be proven. Google image it, although I am 39 now, you can still tell that it is me. The image shows what I end up looking like after an REM driven clone gathering with a skeleton popping out from my chest. I understand most of you are going to continue reading because although it is "liberating", it is also "paralysing" at the same time (Laurence Mountford) to realise what the truth of the world is, so I will display two images below, but promise yourself, that you will Google search this image in your spare time.

Image 3: Megadeth Album Cover: *The World Needs a Hero* (2001)

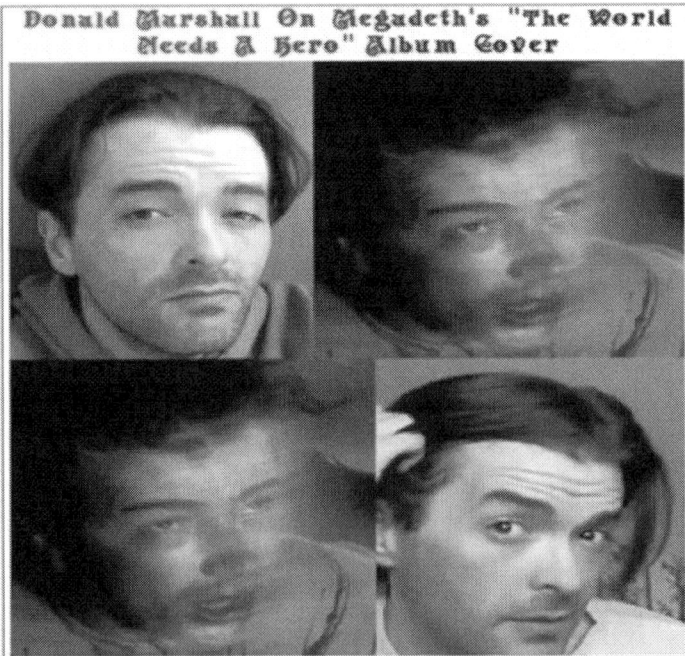

Image 4: My original body: top left (age 37) and bottom right (age 37);
compared to my 23 year old REM driven duplicate clone body (top right and bottom left)
at the cloning centre.

You can clearly see from the images that, it is in fact me. In Image 4, you can also compare what my real body (top left and bottom right) looks like compared to my duplicate clone body. Duplicate clones do not come out of the tank looking 100% like the original; it's 99% - there are always some slight variations as some have commented that the eyebrows and nose in the picture, bottom right, is not the same (as the duplicate clone on the album cover). However, to people who make such comments, I say: my eyebrows and nose is the same when you compare it to the pictures of my original body (top left and bottom right). Also, remember that the image on the album cover is a duplicate REM driven clone of me. REM duplicate clones do not come out of the tank looking 100% like the original. There are always slight variations; but the wrinkles on my 37 year old forehead (when I took the picture in my original body; top left and bottom right) is similar to my 23 year old wrinkles, the lips are the same; and the face which you see, is definitely, the same! Yes. REM duplicate cloning is real; going to sleep and waking up as a cloned version of you is real, and **we must put a stop to it now!**

## *The Deplorable Nature of the Illuminati*

My own family has been turned against me one by one. The Illuminati have told my family members when they were REM driven clones at the cloning centre, things such as I secretly hit or molested their children; poisoned their pets when the pets died of sickness and other such things to make my own family hate me and not want to help me. Even when my family side with me there at the cloning centre, as REM driven clones of themselves; and my family members say 'They do not believe that Donny did all those horrid things' -which they have been told; Elizabeth then says "Are you cooling me a liyah?!" in her disgusting croaking voice made as low as low and evil sounding as she can make it, complete with psychotic and malevolent glare; and as terrified REM driven clones my family say "No, no, of course [what you are saying] it's true", stuttering and afraid as REM clones. My mother Catherine McMahon sold me into this REM driven sex and torture cloning slavery when she remarried a man named Gordon Cohoon; Gordon's whole family is in this scummy secret society, his brothers Tom and Tony Cohoon; his sisters Darlene and Bernadette Cohoon; they fear the new and improved lie detector tests; and all it would take, is for an independent source, far, far removed from any association with the Illuminati to administer these lie detector tests on me **AND** the above named people to prove this unequivocally.

Half way through the making of my original disclosure document (in **2011**), when I went to sleep that evening, the Illuminati transferred my consciousness to my REM driven clone and introduced me to a man (who was also a REM driven clone) named TROY LANDRY. He is an alligator trapper from Louisiana on the TV program named "Swamp People". Troy Landry said "If I send my [original] disclosure out to the public then he would take a power drill to my shin bone at the cloning centre and suck the marrow from my [REM driven clone's] bones." It is similar to spinal tap, and one of the WORST things you can do to a REM driven clone besides burning a REM driven clone. I told Troy that I will be sending out my disclosure to the public, because I have to escape the cloning centre, and so, Troy Landry did just that. It was excruciatingly painful; all the REM driven clones that were sitting in the stands of the arena just watched; slack-jawed. Troy Landry is an insatiable child molester and an extra retarded REM driven clone. A side effect of REM driven cloning is that, as a REM driven clone version of yourself, your emotions are heightened and you are less smart as you are when you are experiencing the world in your original body. Nevertheless, Troy Landry is extra retarded as a REM driven clone.

In Louisiana, when Troy sees a young boy that he likes, Troy asks of the boy's name and tells the boy "He is an alligator hunter"; Troy then proceeds to shake the boy's hand; Troy then has his paedophile friends at the local cloning centre find the boy's blood records to grow duplicate clones of the boy. Five months later, there are multiple REM driven duplicate clone bodies of the boy grown for Troy Landry to victimise before the crowd of onlookers. All members of the Illuminati do this; it's just a way of life to them; they consider themselves 'the privileged people' in the world power organisation. Almost all the cast on the "Swamp People" television program attended the cloning centre as REM driven duplicate clones of themselves, **when they go to sleep**. After putting a power drill to my shin bone, Troy Landry asked me again, "Will I send my [original] disclosure out?" I said "Yes" to which he replied "I'll do the same to your pelvic bone everyday!" The pain on my pelvic bone was far worse than when Troy put the power drill to my REM driven clone shin bone. I told Troy "I have no choice but to inform the public" – and so Troy put a power drill to my REM driven pelvic bone, everyday... and it is the worst pain ever... you forget your own name; where you are; all you know is pain; and you beg God or anything to save you from it...

Another deplorable thing which the Illuminati did in real life is: The Canadian government were trying to lower the amount of prostitutes on the streets (Elizabeth hates prostitutes) so they had a man named Robert Pickton start killing the women and feeding the women to pigs on his farm. The Illuminati had a camera set up in the upper corner of a room in Pickton's house and recorded Pickton hitting these women over the head with a hammer (a ball-peen hammer). They took the recordings, all 49 of these murders, and they all watch them at the cloning centre. To be seen as 'tough' at the cloning centre is to watch all 49 of the Pickton murders without having it affect your psyche. Elizabeth loves watching the Pickton murders and she says she has a macabre fascination with death. Canadian Prime minster Steven Harper knows all about the conduct of the Pickton murders; he has seen all the recordings and cheers on as the rest of them do. If Mr. Pickton says anything about his involvement with the Illuminati, or the recordings, they will apply a constant electrical current to his REM driven clone until Pickton has a heart attack or aneurysm in his original body.

### *What Happened to Britney Spears?*

The Pickton murders are also the reason Britney Spears 'lost it' and shaved her head bald. She had watched too many Pickton murders as a REM driven clone at the cloning centre and it drove her 'over the edge'. I'll also reference the following songs performed by Britney Spears so that the reader has more corroborating evidence to add to the ever increasing pile. Search for the video "Break the Ice" (BritneySpearsVevo 2009) on YouTube. In the Japanimation video; at the beginning of the video; that is a cloned **cartoon** version of Britney Spears being grown in a big thick thank full of water (1 second to 7 seconds); and at 1:32 min to 1:43 min Britney walks into the cloning centre. This is **EXACTLY** how the cloning tubes are in real life. They are stacked one on top of the other, each filled with salty water. Britney Spears made this video because she said a fantasy of hers is to "Blow up a cloning centre". The Illuminati allowed her to release this video because at the time they figured nobody would ever figure it out. I have provided the images on the next page.

Image 5: Britney Spears is being grown as a duplicate clone in a cloning tube. The depiction is EXACTLY how the duplicate clones are grown in the Cloning Centre... with wires extending from the body; in a big thick tank full of salty water.

Image 6: Britney Spears walks into the cloning centre. The cloning tubes are stacked one on top of another. This is EXACTLY how these cloning tubes are in real life at the Cloning Centre.

Image 7: The Cloning Centre depicted from an aerial view.

In "Hold it Against Me" (BritneySpearsVevo 2011) performed by Britney Spears; Britney is depicted fighting against her clone at 2:46 min till the end of the video. In "Mona Lisa" (SimpleGirl4ewer 2007) later remade by Britney Spears she changed the words in the song from "gone" to "cloned". I'll provide the lyrics to chorus here because they have not changed it on A-Z lyrics etc., but listen to the song and you will clearly hear the following:

Britney Spears Lyrics "Mona Lisa"

She's the original (yeah, yeah)
She's unforgettable (yeah yeah)
She wants you to know (yeah)
She's been cloned…
It's kind of incredible (yeah yeah)
She's so unpredictable (yeah yeah)
She wants you to know (yeah)
She's been cloned,
She's been cloned,
She's been cloned…

Yes. Britney Spears and many other celebrities want you to know they have been cloned. The celebrities are depending on you, the ordinary man / woman; the populace, as I am depending on you to spread this message fast and far. In fact Elizabeth has said that "If any public person speaks out, they will die!" Therefore, public figures cannot openly discuss this topic to warn the populace –so they hint. It is **NOW** up to the ordinary man and woman to end this. Furthermore, Elizabeth has a nuclear bomb hooked up at the cloning centre which she can press at any time to wreck havoc on the world unsuspectingly. Thankfully, I managed to convince Elizabeth not to do such a silly thing. I hope you can now understand why everyone is terrified of Elizabeth at the cloning centre, and why this is a **world emergency** and we are depending on you to share and spread my disclosure!

## NEVER EVER SELL YOUR SOUL

### In This Physical World Selling Your Soul Is Selling Your REM Driven Clone

Furthermore I must discuss an entrapment many up and coming 'stars' fall into. You have most likely heard many public figures say "I sold my soul to the devil" or some variation of "I sold my soul". I am now going to address the aspect of "selling souls" or "selling your soul" which I am sure you have heard many of these celebrities talk about. I'll address this as coherently as I can, because on the surface, selling your soul talk is difficult to contemplate, especially, if you consider the soul to be a metaphysical, ethereal or mystical part separate from your earth body. Moreover, we live in a physical world, so selling a metaphysical aspect of you sounds incomprehensible (at first). For the most part we have little understanding of what the soul is. However, we are told that the soul is a part of us which never dies and it is eternal. It is all that we are, ever were, and ever will be. Now our faiths and beliefs come into question, because if you are an atheist: there is no God, selling your soul is a bunch of crazy nonsense.

From a practical perspective it also seems difficult to fathom, because if you go on what you have been told, you are selling an intangible part of yourself to be used by someone else for whatever they wish; and so if you get into the headspace of viewing your soul as something separate from you or that you are in control of your mind and your body, then again, 'selling an intangible aspect of you' again sounds like nonsense because right now nobody controls you; you are controlling you; so what are you really selling? Thin air?

Many up and coming 'stars' think this way when they are confronted with "selling their soul" aspect. The up and coming 'stars' are blinded by the prospect of being super famous and super rich; and in the moment they are confronted with "selling their soul" they believe these Illuminati people, are a group of over religious zealots and that they, -the up and coming 'stars' are taking advantage of the Illuminati because the 'soon to be 'stars'' do not believe (in that moment) it is possible to sell your soul, and only consider being super rich and super famous; so the 'stars' sign their 'soul' over.

At this point, it is usually too late for the up and coming 'star'; because what they have actually sold, in this physical world, is the use of their REM driven clone to the Illuminati. They have sold their REM driven clone to be used for REM driven sex by perverse old men and women whenever they enter REM sleep.

These celebrities are not memory suppressed either; so whenever they enter REM sleep, their consciousness is transferred to their REM driven clone, to be used for whatever the Illuminati wish: usually sex as REM driven clones with dirty and perverse old men in return for a promotion in the entertainment industry; such as movie role, advertisements, concert gigs etc. It is a very, very, sick business, and once these up and coming 'stars' get into the business they are trapped. Now you can begin to understand why so many celebrities, although on the surface it appears they have it all, are depressed; and do random and crazy things. It is a cry for help. Their illogical behaviours, (not all) for the most part, can be attributed to REM driven cloning. Furthermore, the Illuminati consider 'selling your soul' (the use of your REM clone) **a very serious business.** They do not joke about this; and there are NO RETURNS. Once you have sold the use of your REM driven clone for promotions etc., that's it. If you ever make a fuss and want your 'soul' back, in other words: you no longer wish to have your REM driven clone to be used by dirty old men for sex; the Illuminati will kill you by applying a constant electric current to your REM driven clone until you have a heart attack or aneurysm in your original body and die. It is as simple as that.

For example, Whitney Houston wanted nothing to do with the cloning centres, she said she would keep quiet; she never wants to be in the spotlight; she never wants to do radio or television. Let bygones be bygones, I'll go my way and you can go your way. The Illuminati were extremely angry! They had bank-rolled her, and now she didn't want to be their 'friend' or ever associate with them again. She was sacrificed; she was killed with a constant electric current to her REM clone. She had sold her soul, in the beginning of her career; in other words, the "use of her REM clone". Earlier in Whitney Houston's career, she had signed that they can use her REM driven clone however they wish.

I have also seen people say "No" –when confronted with 'selling their souls'. These people are then memory suppressed, and will not remember the proposal of their REM driven experience. The people who also refuse to sell the use of their REM driven clone ('sell their souls') are blacklisted secretly, and they will never receive a high paying movie role, concert gig, advertisements etc. If you have ever wondered why so many talented people have not 'made it' –they refused to sell their souls, in other words, the use of their REM driven clones in exchange for promotions. This is how the entertainment industry really works. Another aspect of selling your soul, in other words, **selling your REM driven clone** is that you are also agreeing to sell your children, and your children's children etc.; your whole lineage to the Illuminati; for the Illuminati to use your unborn children for paedophilia, torture, sex sports and other grotesque and ungodly things when they sleep. It is a nasty business. **NEVER EVER** sell your soul.

The lesson is very important. NEVER EVER, 'sell your soul'; NEVER, EVER! You will experience the worst nightmare situation ever, and in this physical world, that is the use of your REM driven clone to be used for sex sports. You'll never have a decent night's sleep ever again, and you will always retain the full memory of your REM driven clone experiences; as well as, you will be selling your unborn children into this dirty business. Even when confronted with this as a joke: never sell your soul. Never Ever! The physical aspect you are confronted with when asked to 'sell your soul' is: "YOU", and everything which makes you, "you"; your ideas, your creativity, your privacy, your biology; everything which makes you, you. Never sell your soul, which in this life is currently the use of your REM driven clone! Never, ever! I hope that is well received.

## *Fake Alien Abductions conducted through REM Driven Cloning Technology*

I must add they grow duplicate REM driven clones of people from all walks of life and then they transfer the persons consciousness to their REM driven clone version at the cloning centre while the person's REM driven duplicate clone is chained down to stainless steel corpse tables; or they pre-inject the REM driven duplicate clones with drugs before transferring the consciousness so that once the consciousness has been transferred, the REM driven clone cannot move. This is the point when they usually send people into the room dressed as aliens. It is a fake alien abduction. It's just these Illuminati people dressed in Hollywood quality accessories and they make the REM driven duplicate clones which have either been chained to the steel corpse tables or pre-injected with drugs, believe they are having an 'alien abduction'. Members of the Illuminati even dye chicken skin grey, and stretch it over a mask for realism and perform "experiments" on the immobile REM driven clones; the perverts anally probe them; they rape their limb bodies and do not suppress the victims memories; so these victims wake up thinking they have been abducted by aliens but in reality, they had their consciousness transferred to their duplicate clone versions when they entered REM sleep and they were violated. The victims do not know where to turn and naturally, they are embarrassed. Some victims even try and do install cameras all around their bedrooms in order to videotape themselves while they sleep; to prove they have been 'taken'; but to no avail they have not been taken; they have been cloned and had their consciousness transferred to their REM driven duplicate copies once they enter REM sleep by the most disgusting perverts in the world. The scum even videotape these 'abductions' to watch later as sick demented porn. These fake abductions are conducted by the Illuminati more often than you can imagine. They just keep doing it to random people over and over and over...

# I am THE Spy for Humanity against the Corruption of the Illuminati

Over the years the Illuminati have offered me: a priceless katana (samurai sword); a rigged jackpot winning lottery ticket; REM driven clone slaves to keep me quiet, any of the prettiest women I've ever seen; any girl from high school; Vladimir Putin's daughter; even children; I do the right thing and spit in their REM driven clone faces; jam my fingers into their eyes but they have the technology to turn off the pain sensors of a REM driven clone, and therefore they have their pain receptors turned off as REM clones, while my pain receptors are fully on (sometimes even beyond the threshold of what is normal pain for a human). See the online articles: Science Daily (2014) and RT (2014) which discuss how pain receptors can be turned on and off in humans. Not much will hurt their REM driven clones other than getting dirt or vomit in a wound or bleeding too much. However, they have perfected the science and technology of REM driven cloning and therefore it only takes time and approximately $30 to grow new duplicate clone bodies. I started to smear excrement in their faces as a REM driven clone at the cloning centre in an attempt to deter them; I have **never** handled faeces in my original body, but I do this as a REM driven clone at the cloning centre, and even that does not deter them from their depraved ways. I composed a song which was later performed by "One Republic" referring to it called "All the Right Moves" ("All the right friends in all the right places... All the right moves in all the right faces"). I've made so many songs with MK Ultra technology (Rense 2001; Jim Cristea 2009; Berkley News 2011; Mind-Computer 2012 nature video 2013) and Mind-voice technology (New Scientist 2014; Prigg 2014) it is ridiculous. You see it is very easy to make music using Mind-voice technology; Flo-Rida used Mind-voice technology to produce the song "Whistle" when I first made my original disclosure (in 2011). The song is a taunt at me about my "whistle blowing disclosure" i.e. 'Can Donald blow the whistle? Etc. etc.' The thing is, anyone with a talent for music can make music much easier with the technologies which they have (MK ultra technology; Mind-voice technology); however, the Illuminati made more money from the music I composed, and so over the years, they just kept using me, over and over and over again, for rock, pop, rap, country etc. There are so many people involved in this REM driven cloning business, it is staggering; the organisation is vast. The only things the Illuminati fear are nuclear war; the new and improved lie detector tests and the general populace spreading my DISCLOSURE DOCUMENTS.

For those of you thinking Queen Elizabeth II looks like a kindly little old lady and you still cannot believe that all this is true, although I have provided plenty of evidence to the contrary as well as evidence of her saying "Drop the mother f***ing base" as a REM driven clone on a song track (RainmanJhof 2011); you could not be more wrong. She is the worst human being I have ever seen or heard of. It is so sad to see these REM driven women and children having their consciousness transferred to their REM driven clone duplicates and brought to the centre of the dirt rink, sitting there naked, afraid and crying and raped and beaten for sport, for the rich and famous. REM driven cloned women and children display the most range of emotions, and it is the saddest thing to see there. Therefore, of course I cannot bring myself to be a part of this despite any riches which the Illuminati offer me.

Over the 31 years when I was having my consciousness transferred to my REM driven clone at the cloning centre; Elizabeth, Vladimir and many, many, Illuminati members and cloning centre attendees discussed many topics with me. These Illuminati people, such as Elizabeth and Vladimir, as well as many others confided in me because I had composed songs since I was 5 years old.

For readers struggling with the idea that a 5 year old can compose such wonderful songs at such a young age I will remind you that, it is easier to compose songs with technologies such as MK Ultra and Mind-voice technology. One is only limited by their imagination and creativity. Moreover, research talented children. I won't provide references of talented children here because I want to protect children from the Illuminati, and not have children exploited like I was; and for the readers who are parents; I am sure you know how talented, creative, and imaginative your children are.

Accordingly, since the age of 5, Elizabeth, Vladimir and many others, confided me in me because they thought I was special, and wanted me to hang with them; some of these Illuminati people, I had composed their favourite songs; I was also memory suppressed for many years so they thought it was harmless to tell me everything that exists or is possible. They were trying to impress me and amaze me, and therefore they showed me plenty of their technologies and what they had. They wanted me to me a willing, full Illuminati member; so over the years I feigned interest and pretended to like these Illuminati people, so that I could learn what they do and how they do it. I was looking for a way to block the consciousness transfer to a clone during REM sleep, or hoping they would reveal this part to me; but they did not, and I did not find a method to block the consciousness transfer. However, I bided my time, until I knew just about everything they do; so that I could reveal to the world everything they do; to give humanity a fighting chance against everything they do and as a consequence, I became a spy for humanity against the corruption of the Illuminati.

## *The Threat to Humanity when the H.A.A.R.P Grid is Complete*

One of the most important topics which they discussed with me that I must add to this disclosure is HAARP technology and their plans for HAARP technology. I have discussed the basics of HAARP above. HAARP radio transmitters have to be placed at certain points across earth to complete a 'HAARP grid'. Once all the installations are completed over the earth HAARP will have more functions as a grid than the basics described. The Illuminati have told me, there is a possibility the HAARP grid will be capable of time travel, although there is a 50/50 chance using HAARP for time travel could destroy the earth. They also told me that once the HAARP installations are completed, the HAARP grid will be able to bend space and make the distance between, for example, Earth and Pluto approximately 1000 miles for a few seconds, and then the distance will go back to normal.

The Illuminati also said, once the HAARP grid is completed, they would be able to mind control people like never before without the use of RFID microchips or MK Ultra. Life on earth will be much worse once all the HAARP installations are up and working together in unison. The grid has to be complete though. HAARP cannot achieve time travel manipulation and mind control if it is just located in one or a few locations around the earth. There must be a certain number of HAARP installations around the world, in certain locations around the world; and the HAARP radio transmitters must be working in unison in order to achieve time travel manipulation and mind control of the populace of earth.

This is what they told me as REM driven clones at the cloning centre. This disclosure could be false, or a half truth. I do not know. However, it is very important that I add this to the disclosure because the Illuminati are working twice as fast to complete the HAARP grid to achieve their aim of mind control over the entire population since the time I sent out my first disclosure (in **2011**). Whether or not they will achieve their aim of total mind control once all the HAARP installations are completed is NOT something we can afford to debate. They also told me that once the HAARP installations are completed; they will have the capability to mind control anyone remotely, like never before, at the push of a button. HAARP will also be capable of setting back time; which the Illuminati will use if they are ever in danger of being exposed. However, the Illuminati will remember the previous time, and the general populace will NOT remember the previous time, so that the Illuminati can correct the mistake(s) which led to their downfall. **Once the HAARP grid is completed, humanity will be slaves forever.** This is why we cannot afford to debate. Furthermore, from the book "Angels don't play this HAARP" (Begich & Manning 1997, p. 8), it is estimated that the HAARP grid will be completed by approximately 2017; others estimate by the year 2020. The important thing to note is that humanity does not have long, until the HAARP grid is completed.

I must also add the positive side of HAARP, because as I have said, there is nothing inherently evil about technology. Technology is just a tool; it depends on the person using it. HAARP used correctly, and in the hands of honest men and women, will tame the weather with no adverse effects. Therefore humanity is on a timeline and a deadline to bring the Illuminati to an end. **HAARP is one of the main reasons, this disclosure must spread, and spread fast.**

See below for possible HAARP locations around the earth (Rense 2011). The HAARP sites are located globally where the richest mineral belts are located. Sub-surface mineral exploration has been done from satellites by radio tomography that is 100% accurate.

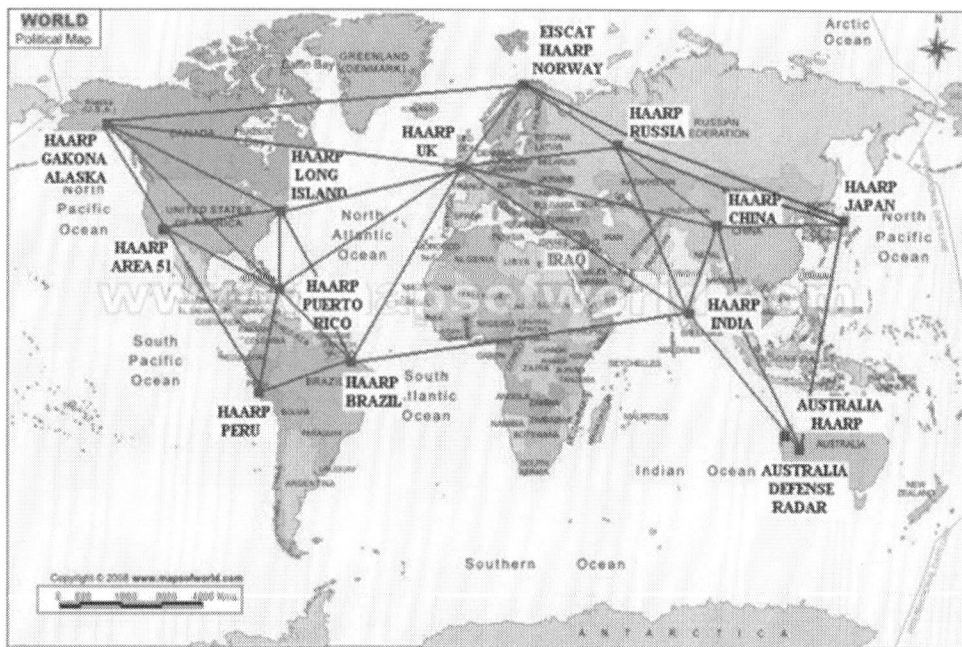

Image 8: Possible H.A.A.R.P. Locations. Source: Rense (2011)

# REM Driven Cloning is the Most Terrible Nightmare Situation Ever

Furthermore, in terms of REM driven cloning; Fefe Dobson (singer) and Kurt Russell (actor) told me during my original disclosure (**2011**) specifically, to include in my disclosure that they do not like the cloning centre and they didn't torture me. Then they said not to mention them, but I will mention them again. Mila Kunis (actress) from "That 70s Show" stabbed in my REM driven clone body multiple times when I made my original disclosure and I was rendered immobile for saying that "She is a slimy scumbag for hanging with these people" and for also saying "She has enormous eyeballs and looks like a lemur". Mila Kunis (as a REM driven clone at the cloning centre) then begged me not to mention her (in my original disclosure, but I'll mention her again too) and then Mila Kunis said "She doesn't want to go to the clone zone anyway" and the Illuminati then deactivated her consciousness from her REM driven clone body, and she left. Her REM driven clone body went limp at the point where her consciousness was deactivated from it; her REM driven clone body looked 'dead', and she was gone. Some of the privileged people at the cloning centre are allowed **NOT** to have their consciousness transferred to their REM driven, clone duplicate versions (or they attend the cloning centre willingly when they want), but not me. I am an imprisoned slave in the worst nightmare situation. I told Nicole Leone (Madonna) also a REM driven clone at the cloning centre, that I was going to tell everyone that she coerced me to compose songs for her throughout my life (as REM driven clones). Nicole Leone (Madonna) told me VERY specifically to say in my disclosure here "She is not afraid!" and "No one will believe me and nothing will come of this". I beg you to help me prove her wrong.

Moreover, having your consciousness transferred to a REM driven clone alternative inhibits the person's ability to dream for that evening. Although your original body is immobile and asleep in your bed, when they transfer your consciousness you have actually 'woken up' as a REM driven clone version of you at a physical location here on earth; therefore you walk and talk as a clone version of you. You are not dreaming; you are just a REM driven clone for the evening. Furthermore, when the Illuminati restore your memories (as they have with me) or do not suppress the memory of your REM driven cloning experience for the evening (such as with the fake alien abductions), you will remember the experience as 'clear as daylight on a summer's day'; the experience is 'clear as a bell' as life is in your original body.

It is unlike dreaming, where dreams are fuzzy, incoherent and with random conjecture. The Illuminati know this as a fact, and therefore pre-inject the REM driven clones of random unsuspecting civilians for the evening with drugs before they transfer the person's consciousness. They tell the person who has had their consciousness transferred to their REM driven clone all sorts of nonsense: such as they are in the 5th Dimension; the astral plane; a singularity; the spiritual realm; Valhalla; quantum hopping etc., and all sorts of fallacies so that the person will not have a coherent picture of what has happened or what is happening. The truth is that person has had their consciousness transferred to their REM driven duplicate clone when they went to sleep and entered REM sleep; their original body still remains asleep in their bed; their consciousness however is now transferred to a clone duplicate alternative, and the person is 'awake', walking and talking as a cloned version of themselves in a physical location on earth. The Illuminati allow some people to retain some of these REM driven clone experiences to affect their mental psyche.

The physical location where the populace will be able to verify these REM driven clones is somewhere within 5/6 hours drive, in a radius of the Robert Pickton farm, Port Coquitlam, British Columbia, in Canada, somewhere at a remote nature reserve. This is the cloning centre all the rich and famous attend because it is above ground and the rich and famous don't like the 'hospital smell' of underground cloning centres. The above ground cloning centre located in Canada is the cloning centre I have my consciousness transferred to when I sleep. It is guarded by military personnel. There are many cloning centres all over the world; as Phil Schneider (1995; 1996) disclosed as far back as the mid 1990s when he spoke: there were 1477 Deep Underground Military Bases (DUMBs) worldwide and 131 active DUMBs in the United States alone. Each DUMB costs on average 17-19 billion U.S. dollars; paid for by the taxpayer; and it takes approximately a year-and-a-half to 2 years to build DUMBs with sophisticated methods. DUMBs contain cloning floors, and have an entire floor dedicated to human cloning, where duplicate clones are grown of unsuspecting civilians (remember they just need your blood / DNA); and unsuspecting civilians have their consciousness transferred to their REM driven clones at a physical location, which is usually these Deep Underground Military Bases when they sleep; unsuspecting civilians are memory suppressed, also to be used for gruesome torture and sex sports; as well as the plagiarism of talented individuals. Schneider gave the above statistics in the mid 1990s; chances are there are more DUMBS and cloning centres worldwide today.

Are you beginning to understand why this is the worst nightmare situation ever? Can you understand how: you, your friends, your family, your brothers, your sisters, aunties, uncles, children, work colleagues and anyone else you have contact with in your network, may be involved in this REM driven cloning business and will not even be fully aware of the situation or remember any experiences which they may have had once they wake up from sleep and they are back in their original bodies? I remember all of the REM driven clone experiences as clear as daylight because my memories are fully restored. Can you understand why the Illuminati must be stopped and stopped immediately? This REM driven clone business is vast, and it affects everyone, not just me.

This is why I mention that I am fortunate or unfortunate to remember all these experiences clearly depending on how you view it. I am unfortunate in the sense that I can recall all the depraved things these people do as REM driven cloned duplicates as clear as daylight and it affects my mental psyche. However, the fortunate part is: because I can recall all these experiences clearly, I can inform the world about the evil committed against humanity in a clear and logical way for the average reader to understand and verify, so that the populace can bring these people to justice for the crimes they have perpetrated against humanity and continue to inflict on humanity. For anyone who has had their intellectual property stolen by the Illuminati as a consequence of the technologies they have used on you unsuspectingly, you will be able to sue and regain monetary reward for the theft of intellectual property as well as invasion of your privacy.

I do not want to get too far ahead, because at this present moment, it is **very important** (I cannot say it enough) that this disclosure spreads (this is the stage we are currently at); it reaches the armed forces; to enable the armed forces to realise the crimes committed against humanity because of these people (the armed forces are kept 'out of the loop'; they just 'follow orders'); the armed forces will have to perform a military coup and bring this people to their knees. This is the point where the ordinary man / woman can have his REM driven cloning experiences restored, (that is if you want to) and sue / rightfully reclaim damages and legal reward for any crimes committed against him or her.

## *The Meek Shall Inherit the Earth*

As you can see if everything goes smoothly; the meek shall inherit the earth. This is why you must maintain your composure and resolve, as I do every single day. You must not riot or cause chaos, damage property or undertake any act which will cause public dissension. The good people of this earth are about to inherit the earth; under no circumstance must you destroy anything. At the end of this currently dire and complicated situation; humanity will inherit the cure for HIV/AIDS, cancer, Alzheimer's, dementia, you name it –many debilitating diseases known to man; and other such wonderful technologies like hypersonic trains which run on magnets and are capable of doing Mach 5 (Mach 5 is the equivalent of 3806 miles per hour or 6125 kilometres per hour; Schneider (1995; 1996) also mentions the availability of Mach 5 trains in his disclosure, back in the 1990s). These trains can be used to deliver foods which are discarded in More Economically Developed Countries (MEDCs) to Less Economically Developed Countries (LEDCs) because these trains can travel thousands of miles within minutes. Yes. The Illuminati have all these wonderful technologies and more, but withhold it, and in turn withhold the progress of humanity. Yes. Plenty of man's problems can be solved when we address the root causes of our problems, and one of the root causes of humanity's problems is: REM driven human cloning which is currently in the hands of evil men. Even REM driven cloning can be used for the benefit of mankind when this tool is in the hands of righteous men. It can be used learn new skills in your sleep: such as gain extra qualifications; learn how to speak a new language; play instruments etc. –so long as memories are not suppressed, you will be able to perform the skills you learned as a REM clone in your original body when you wake up. As you see there is nothing wrong with most technologies; it all depends on the person / people using it. Nevertheless, although they may be beneficial uses to REM driven cloning not yet realised, we must be shut down REM cloning before we can even consider how REM driven cloning may benefit mankind, because at this present moment all that REM driven human cloning is used for is to commit evil, particularly against unsuspecting civilians.

It is OK to feel angry about all these crimes committed against humanity daily. But do not let these evil crimes rule you, in fact, let it motivate you; let it motivate you to the point where you will stand up and speak out to ensure that these crimes end. I think about the children and the future of the world every day; that is what motivates me and I view my situation as a God-given mission to bring these people to justice. I view things this way to maintain my sanity and composure. This is what keeps me going despite the extreme evil I experience, and it helps me to maintain my resolve and composure. The fact that I do not want a single child to grow up in a world, where they are being messed with in their sleep is what keeps me going despite this extreme evil. Some children are even kidnapped and brought to the cloning centre in their original bodies, again to be messed with. This is the root cause of why so many children go missing across the world. I'm sure any rational thinking human being feels the same way I do, and does not want their children, or any child to inherit a sick world governed by sick individuals.

I am a baptised Roman Catholic and a God fearing man. I believe there is a Creator of the universe but the Illuminati tell me there is no God, only science and technology. The Illuminati are also responsible for the death of the young beauty pageant girl Jean-Benet Ramsay; her parents are in this REM driven cloning business. Casey Anthony's daughter; as well as, Casey Anthony (before she died) AND Casey Anthony's parents also attend the cloning centre as REM driven clones. Many others; a man had his wife killed and this was mentioned on the news; it was an Asian woman whose rich husband had killed her; the husband said the wife was responsible for their son's death. Elizabeth's response was that "Rich people in this organisation [The Illuminati] do not go to jail, they are covered for."

Stephen Spielberg and George Lucas are Illuminati members and they willing attend the cloning centre as REM driven clones when they sleep. George Lucas made other Illuminati members light my REM driven clone body on fire for the end of his movie *Star Wars Episode III: Revenge of the Sith* (2005). George Lucas said (as a REM driven clone) he wanted Hayden Christensen "To scream realistically". Hayden Christensen (also a REM driven clone at the cloning centre) watched me, and listened to my screams and groans of pain and copied the sounds coming from my burning REM driven clone exactly. Hayden Christensen knows he is a REM driven clone when he goes to sleep and Hayden Christensen knows his consciousness is transferred when he reaches REM sleep. Hayden Christensen knows all about REM driven human cloning, and he is a "privileged" Illuminati member. Natalie Portman also knows all there is to know about REM driven human cloning; as does approximately a quarter of the "Star Wars" cast. Many directors have attended the cloning centre as REM driven clones too, and have used me in a similar role playing situation; they have caused me to have excruciating pain as a REM driven clone, to see what kind of squeak or screech I will make, as if I were less than a dog; and when I am a bloody mess on the floor as a REM driven clone; that is when they usually crawl on my broken REM driven clone body and sodomize me saying something like "They love me and they cannot control themselves because I made all their favourite songs and I'm so "special"".

My ribs in my REM driven clone body will be broken, I will have suffered internal bleeding and will be crying or screaming, if I am able, but they just continue to sodomize me, and videotape such a depraved act of wickedness so that they can view it again like "evil pornography".

The REM driven cloned children, who have their consciousness transferred while they sleep at home in bed, in their original bodies, need a familiar face to talk to as REM clones or all they do is scream and cry at the cloning centre; that is where Joy Geizer comes in. Joy Geizer is married to my half brother from my father's first marriage; Joy Geizer is a REM driven clone girl guide leader, and when the Illuminati clone young girls, Joy Geizer speaks to these REM driven cloned girls; Joy Geizer keeps the REM driven cloned girls calm and "pimps" them out for free, knowing that these young girls will have their memories suppressed, and therefore they will not remember the experience and will not talk about it when they wake up. All the Geizers are in this REM driven, human cloning business; there are many people who remember these REM driven cloning experiences in their 'awake state' and in their original bodies who could be polygraph tested by independent polygraph testers. The police, and polygraph testers in my City of Halifax, Nova Scotia are compromised (they attend cloning centres as REM driven clones too); they cover up for child molesters and therefore cannot be trusted to fairly administer a polygraph test; as I said, commissionaires and C.S.I.S are heavily involved. All it would take is a few polygraph tests to prove these things unequivocally, because for those of you who have 'eyes', you can already see that REM driven cloning is real, and that this is actually the way of the world. I will take these polygraph tests publicly too, and demand that my mother and step father submit to them. They have told me, they **wouldn't** even attempt to lie on a polygraph.

Human cloning, particularly REM driven human cloning, is one of the absolute truths of this world; hidden from the world for over 70 years. My life and the freedoms of many, many people, including the reader (you) depend on this disclosure. The Illuminati say that the world finding out about REM driven human cloning will set the stage for the end of the world; people panicking and destroying property because of the evil these people have committed, but as I've said: prove them wrong, because we are going to inherit the earth, so there is no need to riot or cause public dissension. There will be no end of this world; just the end of the crazy Illuminati people. They always like to think and behave so negatively, don't they? *Sigh*. Furthermore, the whole talk about 2012; December 21$^{st}$ 2012 and the end of the world Mayan Prophecy; that was really about the world finding out REM driven human cloning, and the sick and sadistic nature it has been used for by these sick and sadistic people. Under no circumstance must you riot; you **must** prove you are better than these savage barbarians. I'll say it again, **because it is important**: we are going to inherit the earth, and therefore the smart and right thing to do, is not to destroy anything, especially the earth which you shall inherit.

Furthermore, I hope you are beginning to understand that the good people of this world must bring these people to justice and stop their wicked ways. I sincerely wrote this disclosure so that the good people of earth would be empowered to put a stop to their wicked ways. I wrote this disclosure to empower the good people of earth against tyranny and not so that the world would end. Therefore you must understand that the downfall of these Luciferians (Illuminati) must progress smoothly, because unless you have been to the cloning centre as a REM driven clone and retained the full memories of your experience, it is difficult to understand the level of depravity and sub human cruelty; it is beyond anything that has ever been heard of, and there is much more to tell.

Ignore this disclosure and you will condemn me to a horrible eventual death and you will encourage them that 'they are all 'powerful''. This is not an exaggeration. There is no need to exaggerate; even President Barrack Obama is involved in the REM driven cloning business and attends the cloning centre as a REM driven clone version of himself, when he goes to sleep. He and his wife Michelle Obama attend these REM driven clone gatherings. Barrack Obama has even told me as a REM driven clone, at the cloning centre "Donny, we're all powerful. You are a slave and the people here [as REM driven clones at the cloning centre] won't speak up for you for fear of torture or death. Now make us a new song or we'll gut you like fish and leave you to writhe in agony!"

## *Be Wary of: Shills; Trolls; Disinformation Agents and Double Agents*

There are many, many disinformation agents whose aim it is, is to denounce or debunk me. Be very wary of them. They DO NOT, and cannot debunk me, because after all, everything I have disclosed is truth. Although the truth concerns highly advanced concealed technologies, so it is a bit difficult to fathom at first, but keep reading, and you will realise that all which I have disclosed is true. Be very wary of the disinformation agents.

The most common thing these people say is that "Donald is a paranoid schizophrenic" –yet, ask them to detail the ins and outs of what a paranoid schizophrenic is and what specifically qualifies Donald to be a 'paranoid schizophrenic'; there is a high probability they will not be able to explain this to you, logically, sequentially and methodologically. Their main goal is just to make it as difficult for newcomers to understand what the real truth of this world is and as I have disclosed; and one of the root causes of man's problems is REM driven cloning.

Some disinformation agents are paid by the Illuminati, to behave this way, and are all too happy to echo empty statements (without any substantial evidence for their claims) because it provides them with a pay check. I will provide the following reference for the reader which discusses the signs and symptoms of a paranoid schizophrenic; all for the express intent for the reader to further understand paranoid schizophrenia. You can read more about paranoid schizophrenia on Medical News Today (2015). The link is provided in the reference section. You are welcome to read my Facebook wall and within days, you will realise I converse with others quite naturally. You can also ask individuals who have spoken to me through Skype or met me; but if this is not a viable option for you; all you have to do is read my Facebook wall and within days, you'll see that whoever makes such harsh and untrue remarks on my character is in fact a disinformation agent.

Furthermore, remember we live in a 3D **physical** world; and there is always a physical aspect to how something manifests. Therefore, when you hear others discussing concepts such as 'Tila Tequila demonstrated an 'energy ball' right on camera; why didn't Donald discuss that?!' Please understand that these people are trying to deceive you with misinformation. There are also professional disinformation agents to be wary of. I do not perceive anything extra-ordinary in the world when I am awake in my original body beyond the five senses. I don't see orbs, auras or anything of the like. All I will ever discuss are practical things which have been unequivocally proven to me as fact; because in the situation the earth is currently in, I cannot afford to speculate.

## *Contact Information*

My Facebook is: https://www.facebook.com/donald.marshall.148
You can also press Ctrl+Click (hold "Ctrl" on your keyboard and left "Click" with your mouse, on the image to your right).

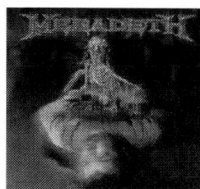

I have a public wall on Facebook which starts from March 2012. In other words, all posts are made public since March 2012 and you do not have to join my friends list or subscribe me to see what I post (although you will have to have a Facebook account). I suggest that newcomers start reading from March 2012, and be patient, and read everything. You can read everything and learn the real truth of the world free of charge. I don't wish to write a book, I am not looking to turn a profit from this; I want to crush these guys and shut down the cloning centres!

It also worthwhile to add that: I am **not** asking for donations. I do not want **ANY** donations. Ever! These disclosures are far more important than any donations. This is **NOT** my job. I have a job. I am an independent contractor; carpentry is my trade and I earn a living this way. If you sincerely want to help; the best way to help is to spread and share my disclosures. That is all I ever ask for, so that eventually, the world knows about REM driven human cloning, and the armed forces can bring these people to their knees. **That is all I want; spread, spread, and spread this disclosure.** I will **never ever** ask for donations. Ever! Please keep this in mind, and anyone who asks for donations in my name or on my behalf should not be trusted. I, Donald Marshall, will **NEVER EVER** ask for any donations. I hope that is well received.

You can also view Proboards which has all my Facebook posts and have been archived by Celine O'Carroll and Astral 7ight by visiting:

http://donaldmarshall.proboards.com/
You can also press Ctrl+Click (hold "Ctrl" on your keyboard and left "Click" with your mouse, on the image to your right).

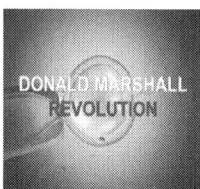

There is a search function on Proboards, and you can use this to search for and read all the disclosures I have made regarding REM driven clones, the people involved and more. I understand that it is human nature to want to know, which people have been to the cloning centre as REM driven clones; therefore, use the search function to read about any public figure which I have already covered that you have an inkling about. You can also post anonymously on Proboards and Celine and other Administrators will transfer your question onto Facebook which I'll answer.

Donald Marshall Revolution is a website which details a brief overview of the Illuminati. http://donaldmarshallrevolution.com/
You can also press Ctrl+Click (hold "Ctrl" on your keyboard and left "Click" with your mouse, on the image to your right).

## *Interviews*

You can listen to the radio interviews I have done. Listen for consistency; particularly anything which you do not hear me, pronounce clearly for the first time; the best thing to do is to pause the recording at that particular point and replay it. You should also research the statement you do not understand. Sometimes reading helps comprehension a lot faster.

One of the main reasons you should pause and replay the recordings is because: the truth has been kept hidden for so long that a lot of what I discuss in my interviews are beyond most people's current world view; so at some points I may speak too fast for you; my audio/ microphone may not be so clear so you may miss what I say etc.

A friend has told me that when he first watched the Vinny Eastwood interview; he did not hear me say the word "scars" (When Vinny asked: 'How do I know I'm the real me?') although he replayed that particular point in the video 8 times. Everything was just beyond his current comprehension, at the time. No matter how many times he replayed that part he really could not hear me say the word "scars" –so he let that part go, and played the rest of the interview, pausing, and replaying points which he did not understand, especially to comprehend whether I was talking about my original body or my REM driven clone duplicate body. He also listened to all my interviews for consistency, to note any 'slip ups', or any parts of my testimonies which do not 'add up'. He would listen to all my interviews, pausing and replaying parts he did not understand and he would reserve his judgements until he felt everything I was saying was for example as ordinary as: 'I woke up today, brushed my teeth, and took the dog for a walk'. He was also patient to realise the truth. After listening to my interviews he would just let it 'sink in'. A week later he would come back and listen to the same interviews, to test whether his comprehension on the topics I discuss has improved, and whether he can understand what I am saying without having to pause and repeat at certain points in my interview; and soon enough he could now hear me say "scars" at that particular point of the Vinny Eastwood interview. He had reached the point where all topics I discuss sounded to him like I'm saying everyday common place stuff that people have heard, such as: 'I woke up today, brushed my teeth, and took the dog for a walk'. For anyone who may struggle to understand the topics I discuss: I strongly recommend you take the above approach as my friend did; soon enough, you too will realise the real truth of the world like he has: REM driven cloning, kept secret and used for sinister purposes.

I cannot say the following is true for everybody, however, an unproductive venture a complete newcomer can do is to listen to my interviews first time, all the way through, without pausing or replaying parts which they do not fully understand; If you do this and if there is just a single part of my interviews which does not make sense to you; this will interfere with your understanding of the entire interview. Remember, all I am discussing is technology, thousands of years advanced compared to what you currently use; available today, hidden and secret. If things start to get too complex for you, reduce it to its bare minimums: (advanced) science and technology. I hope that helps.

Another thing which I do in my interviews, that friends have picked up on, is:- because REM driven cloning has been my reality for many years; I don't differentiate between my original body and my REM driven clone body. I just say: I did this, I did that, and Elizabeth did this and that, therefore it can become very confusing for newcomers. Please bare with me; although I'm more emotional as a REM driven clone, and not as smart as I am in my original body (this is a side effect of cloning: REM driven clones are more emotional than normal, and dumber than they are in their original bodies) I'm still "me" when my consciousness is transferred; I have all the experiences and knowledge which makes me, "me" and therefore I naturally do not differentiate between my REM driven clone version, and my original body as an outsider discussing these concepts would. I understand it helps comprehension so I have painstakingly done this throughout this disclosure.

I hope this helps; and I hope this helps to better understand my disclosure as well as the interviews which I have done. On the next page you can find the links to my interviews. You can copy and paste the links to your web browser or press Ctrl+Click – (hold "Ctrl" on your keyboard and left "Click" with your mouse, on the images below) to direct you to the interviews.

# Links to Donald Marshall Interviews

## Vincent Eastwood

Copy and paste the link below to your web browser.
https://www.youtube.com/watch?v=M_1UiFeV5Jg&ab_channel=VincentEastwood
OR Press Ctrl+Click (on the image below) to follow the link.

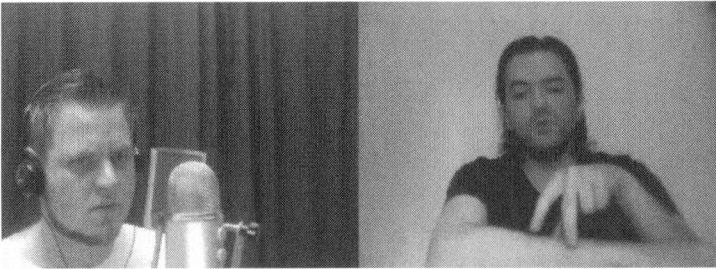

## Jeanice Barcelo

Copy and paste the link below to your web browser.
https://www.youtube.com/watch?v=3uzgu4ekT3c&ab_channel=JeaniceBarcelo
OR Press Ctrl+Click (on the image below) to follow the link.

## Lisa Phillips (CFR)

Copy and paste the link below to your web browser.
https://www.youtube.com/watch?v=UonnFuHLJKc&ab_channel=Astral7ight
OR Press Ctrl+Click (on the image below) to follow the link.
Listen to parts 1 through 8.

## Radio Presenters –Contact Donald Marshall

Anyone who sincerely wants to contact me for radio interviews on their show is welcome to do this. Please contact me through Proboards by leaving a message for me to contact you.

## Professionals who understand "Consciousness Transfer" –Contact Donald Marshall

Any neuroscientists, engineers or professionals who understand how consciousness transfer works, and can provide me with a detailed methodology of how to block the consciousness transfer to my REM driven clone; please message me on Proboards, and this will be greatly appreciated.

## Email

I currently do not have a contactable email address. In my original disclosure, the email address has been compromised (hacked), and so has any other email accounts I created: Yahoo, hotmail, Gmail, AOL etc. It doesn't matter; they eventually get hacked; for whatever reason, the Illuminati do not want me to have an email account.

## How to Learn More about Donald Marshall's Whistle Blowing Disclosures

The best ways to learn about the truth of the world is through my Facebook page and Proboards. There is a mountain of evidence which has been collated over the years, and corroborates all that I have disclosed here. I also understand that for some people it is impractical to read three years worth of Facebook posts, especially when some post are repetitive; contain unnecessary comments from trolls, shills and other disinformation agents. Therefore, I am currently compiling 5 documents which should make it easier for others to read and understand everything quickly; as well as, for others to share and spread those 5 documents including this main disclosure document –so 6 documents about the real truth of the world. All for free!!

These documents include:
- "Frequently Asked Donald Marshall Questions" –This will contain all the general FAQs which I have been asked over the years; all in one place.
- "Experiences from the cloning centre" –This document will contain the full disclosure of my REM driven cloning experiences from the cloning centre when I go to sleep; all in chronological order.
- "List of people to avoid" This will contain a whole list of trolls, shills, and disinformation agents and double agents in alphabetical order, to avoid at all costs, in real life and online; -all complied in one place; and the reasons why they should be avoided.
- "Public Figures and their relationship with Donald Marshall as REM driven clones" – this will be a complete list of every public figure I have ever come into contact with as a REM driven clone; and you will be able to read about all the public figures I have met as REM clones, as well as the experiences, all in one place.
- "The subterranean underground colonists: The Vril" –this will be everything about the biological parasites the Illuminati harbour. Yes. The Illuminati harbour biological parasites, which they use against unsuspecting humans. I told you the Illuminati were

the biggest depraved perverts ever to grace God's earth. REM driven human cloning, kept secret from the world for over 70 years is difficult to fathom as it is, as are these biological parasites. These parasites are also one of the main root causes of humanity's problems here on earth, and must be rendered extinct. In this document you will be able to learn everything about their, strengths, weaknesses, psychology, biology, ecology, sexuality and arm yourself with knowledge which ensures that humanity exterminates these parasites from our earth, forever. The secret of Vril; a secret no more!

I hope after reading my eye witness statements presented in this document that you have now began to understand that this is simply what is happening in our world today.

Heed my disclosure, very diligently. At the start of my disclosure I asked the reader to do two things:

1) Give me the benefit of the doubt –because there is nothing worse than being a victim of abuse, reporting it and the people who have the power to stop it, ignore you;
2) Set out on a genuine quest to debunk my disclosure. I understand that for some people, plenty of what I have disclosed will still sound 'too out there' beyond their current scope of reality to be believable. For such people, the honest thing to do is to start with the first topic which you do not fully understand and explore it, either by finding that corresponding topic on Proboards (Donald Marshall Proboards 2015), and continuing your research from there; or just Google any topic you currently do not understand and review the  topic on websites such as New Scientist (2015), Gizmag (2015), Motherboard (2015), BBC News (2015a; 2015b), BBC Future (2015), The Guardian (2015a; 2015b) The Independent (2015a; 2015b), Daily Mail Online (2015) and start reading more articles in the Science and Technology columns because these people have been telling you what they have been doing for decades. Consequently, keep in mind that articles which discuss 'future' technologies and 'improvements' in medicine or science, are articles, which are **really** discussing present technologies, and achievements in science and medicine already realised; because most of these achievements have been realised decades ago. It just hasn't been fully disclosed publicly.

**I have also saved and backed-up every reference (except the homepages of the websites referenced) in this document; therefore if a link or video is ever deleted let me know.**

## *How Much Do You Know About Post-humanism / Trans-humanism?*

Furthermore, you have to be honest here: because if you do not know much or anything about post-humanism / trans-humanism then I am afraid to say, -and this is no fault of yours –that you are behind in this the world; simply because these Illuminati people are Post-humanists; and that is the direction the want the rest of the world to go. They want the world to reach a destination where human cloning is common place; a world where downloading your mind / entire life experience onto a computer microchip and living on as a cloned version of you with the microchip running the consciousness to be common place; and these Illuminati Post-humanists want the world to head in a direction where it is commonplace to molest children through science and technology. No. This really is not Science-Fiction, this is the world we live in today; this is why such marvels in science, medicine and technology has been withheld from the general public and kept hidden by an 'elite' group of people because if these people honestly came forward, and said "We have invented this technology and we want to use it for this "negative" purpose" –the populace would not accept it, and these people will be lynched in the streets before lunchtime. Therefore, through concealed advancements in medicine, science and technology, the Illuminati can live out their inner depraved cravings and commit crimes against humanity and the world, for which most people will be too blind to see or even fathom, because the hidden science and technology is beyond the average person's current comprehension.

Therefore, please attain an education in post-humanism / trans-humanism because these Illuminati people believe they can rival creation, nature and the marvels of the universe through science, medicine and technology. The Illuminati go **against** creation; they go **against** nature; and they go **against** humans. They don't consider themselves humans. They consider themselves post-humans and believe they can become "gods" through advancements in medicine, science and technology. See LawOfIdentity (2014) and Mark Dice (2014) for Richard Seed's comments on 'becoming gods' through transhumanism. Richard Seed is a Physicist with a Ph.D. from Harvard University; he is well known in the controversial cloning debate and declares his aspirations to "become god" saying 'We are going to become Gods, period. If you don't like it, get off. You don't have to contribute, you don't have to participate, but if you are going to interfere with me becoming a God, you're going to have trouble. There'll be warfare.' If you value humanity, do your best to attain an education in the trend of post-humanism / trans-humanism; otherwise the future of mankind will be bleak. We must do everything we can to stop these people.

This is of uttermost importance. REM driven cloning of is the most terrible thing in the world, especially when it involves unsuspecting civilians, and worst of all, innocent children. If you choose NOT to do anything you allow the Illuminati to continue to clone your children, sisters, wives, and sons. You allow the Illuminati to continue to hijack the minds of your children, sisters, wives, and sons while they sleep, through concealed advancements in science and technology. You allow the Illuminati to transfer the consciousness of your children, sisters, wives and sons to their REM driven duplicate clone versions while they sleep, whereby the Illuminati molest your children, sisters, wives and sons, which will cause them to have learning disabilities, unexplained depression and suicidal thoughts, as well as all kinds of side effects.

## _This IS your ONLY chance to end these monsters. There is a deadline!_

This is your **ONLY** chance to do something to end these monsters. We are on a timeline and there is a deadline. As I have already mentioned, as well as, the top scientists in the field of physics and geophysics have mentioned: HAARP is not only capable of controlling the weather; once the HAARP grid is completed and working at full power, it will be capable of mind control over entire populations. We will all be slaves to the Illuminati FOREVER. Our freewill will be gone forever. Furthermore, if they achieve their aim of time travel with HAARP technology, future generations of humanity will never be able to stop them, because as they have told me: 'They will always be able to go back to a previous time, and correct the mistake(s) which led to their downfall'. This is the Illuminati's end game and what they wish to achieve. This is why this disclosure is so heavy, and so important. It goes beyond REM driven cloning; although it is important the world understands REM driven cloning. The future of humanity is at stake; and because of the 2-5 year deadline until the HAARP grid is completed, it is time humanity stood up and brought an end to the Illuminati. This REALLY is your ONLY chance to end these monsters!

**The only way for evil to triumph is for good people to do nothing.**
**Edmund Burke**

Remember for every 12 months which passes military / concealed technology outstrips the technology the general public is accustomed to by 44 years (Schneider 1995; 1996). Close your eyes and think 44 years into the future. The year is 2059. What kind of technologies do you expect mankind to have? Do it for real; don't just read the words. Close your eyes and imagine. The year is 2059. What kind of technologies does mankind have? You see. It is 'out of this world' technology, right? This is exactly what is going on today in the year 2015. It's just that it is hidden. That's all. Not so difficult to fathom now.

## *Do NOT Be Afraid to Help. We Outnumber the Illuminati by 1,000,000:1*

Don't be afraid to help. These people are easily defeated when good people stand together as one. These Illuminati people total no more than 10,000 people. 10,000 people against 7,000,000,000 (7 billion) people –that's less than 0.000001 % of the world's population. Now can you begin to understand how prevalent evil can be when a small organised group of individuals, as little as 10,000 of the world's most evil and tyrannical people all work together in unison to exert their influence over the world? The world does not have to be this way. We outnumber the Illuminati people by a 1,000,000 to 1. For every Illuminati person there is, there are **one million** people who are not Illuminati, therefore do not to be afraid to help; all you will be doing is helping humanity rid itself of its sickness. So please feel free to share and spread my disclosure far and wide.

For those of you whom this applies to: remember the Illuminati (and I know it sounds ridiculous despite the evil they do) are deeply religious. They believe anyone aiding me is part of the "Army of Light" prophesised by Nostradamus; and to harm or degrade the life of anyone assisting me will bring them to their ultimate end and they will incur the wrath of God; they will suffer utter ruin and demise in their lives if they are to hurt you; they are very scared of people who can see through the lies and deceptions they have inflicted on the world. So please, stay calm, do not stress your heart, and know that **you are safe**, and **they cannot hurt you**. You can feel safe in the knowledge that you can do the right thing by helping me. They told me this as REM driven clones on the night of 21st of February 2014 when I went to sleep. The above is exactly what they said.

For anyone interested in understanding the interpretations of the Nostradamus Prophecies, Crystal Links (2015) provides a good source for all 942 of the quatrains. Delores Cannon is also an author who has written three volumes called "Conversations with Nostradamus" and for anyone interested you can read these online (Galactic 2012a; Galactic 2012b) as well as watch her YouTube videos (CreativeForceVideo 2014; Disclose TruthTV 2015).

Yes. This is the state of the world today: a deception within a deception coated in reverse psychology; and fact is indeed stranger than fiction. Now after everything I have said, if you are still sceptical and 'in-between' on this issue then the best thing for you to do is to pay attention to your dreams; or lack of dreams –they are your own experiences and you cannot deny your experiences.

In other words, you may be having REM driven cloned experiences too; for some people they have a 'dream', where they are in the same environment, over and over and over again; or the theme being discussed in their 'dreams' is the same over and over and over again; or the environment their 'dreams' take place always appear to happen in the same 3 or 4 environments over and over again –no matter what the theme is. In each scenario there is a likely probability that these are not just dreams, and in fact these people have had their consciousness transferred to the REM driven clone duplicates and the Illuminati is trying to extract something from them, once that is done they implant a false memory (See Kim (2013) and Alford (2015) for discussions on how false memories are implanted) so that people wake up with the feeling of remembering something, but in actuality it is false; or the person wakes up with no memory of dreams from the previous evening, which means there is a high probability that person had her / his memories suppressed when her / his consciousness was transferred to her / his REM driven clone. This is why I say you can be sceptical about everything I have said (for now), but pay attention to your dreams, or lack of dreams, they are your own experiences, and you cannot deny your own experiences.

## *Noteworthy Frequently Asked Question*

A Frequently Asked Question I receive, which is worth a mentioning here, is as follows:
**Q**: Donald, if everything you have said is true...; in other words human clones walk among us now in a multilayered conspiracy which reaches the highest levels of government; armed with this knowledge what does one do exactly? What happens now, Donald? You obviously want to spread the word and make people aware but to what end?

**DM**: In short: I want to bring a complete end to the Illuminati and usher in a "Golden Age" of mankind. This question is best answered by detailing my 'Mission and Vision' for ending the Illuminati completely.

## *Donald Marshall's Mission and Vision on How to Bring Down The Illuminati*

- This disclosure must spread, and **spread FAST and FAR!**
- If you now understand everything I have disclosed in this document as truth, then do not waste any more time. Share this disclosure with your wives, husbands, brothers, sisters' aunties, uncles, friends, co-workers, and children. We all have a part to play in saving the world from a premature doom.
- Call friends who have not heard from you in a while and tell them you have important news to share. Share this document. Share it on social media such as Facebook; Twitter; Instagram; Dropbox; Slideshare etc.
- Keep sharing this document until it comes to the attention of the Armed Forces. The Armed Forces will have to intervene. Once the Armed Forces intervene we will have reached the middle stage of this vision and will be witnessing a complete end to the Illuminati. Until then, we're in the beginning stages, so please; spread this document faster and further. The quicker it is spread; the quicker the Illuminati are ended.
- Once the Armed Forces have intervened a Military coup can be orchestrated against these vile people.
- Cloning centres can then be shut down once these people are overthrown.

- The freeing of any missing people (children; teens; adults) trapped in the cloning centres can commence (once the Armed Forces intervene).
- HAARP (as well as other highly advanced technologies) can now be contained and not used for adverse effects against the world (once the world learns of this disclosure).
- These Illuminati people will then HAVE to appear in court for their crimes against humanity.
- Suing the Illuminati members in court (once court proceedings commence... we will be past the midpoint of my vision, and closer towards witnessing a complete end to the Illuminati).
- The populace (and it will be your choice) can then have their REM driven clone experiences restored and also sue and claim any legal reward / compensation.
- After the populace has sued the Illuminati for their crimes against humanity; the punishments can commence.
- Punishments will include: imprisonment and executions of these sick and malevolent people. The imprisonment and executions of evil Illuminati members will bring an end to the Illuminati.
- After the punishments and executions; Governments worldwide can now be replaced with incorrupt individuals, worldwide.
- The structure of Governance will also have to change. The reason for this because future generations will always be able to check their leaders and governance more appropriately; so that the depraved and subhuman acts I describe can NEVER be committed against humanity again; nor will world leaders be capable of committing such monstrous crimes in such secrecy ever again.
- Ensuring that the laws of the land always progresses in line with advancements in medicine, science and technology; as well as, ensuring law progresses in the directions of Research and Development (R&D) regarding future technologies, science and medicine.
- Release of technologies, science and medicine which benefit mankind.
- Commence a "Golden Age" of mankind.

**If you do not fight the corruption and you do not stand up for what is right in life, you end up being a serf and a slave and you are leaving your children a world in which you would not want to live in yourself, so how can you in decency behave that way? You have to stand up for what is right in life, and unless you do that you are nothing.**
**<u>Aaron Russo</u>**

## *<u>Empowerment by Virtue of Golden Truth</u>*

As you can see, despite all the horror of the world I currently present: if everything goes smoothly, the good people of this world, truly will inherit it. This is why despite any anger, sadness, or fears you may have; you must not riot, damage property or cause chaos or bring about any other form of public dissension. You cannot stay silent, or ignore the issue in the hope that the threat removes itself. You are called to act; you must take action to help bring the Illuminati to an end; you must act while at the same time, you must maintain your composure and resolve to ensure that the whole procedure goes smoothly, and we all inherit a world we want to live in.

Your life, **at this very moment**, is more important than you may have probably ever imagined. You have purpose. Through you, and other good people around the world, together we can bring an end to such unspeakable forms of tyranny in this world. It is my humble stance that you have now become truly empowered with golden truth and you are now compelled to bring this tyranny to an end.

Do not waste the knowledge you have obtained from this disclosure. It is my only hope to escape this man made living hell. It is my only hope, as well as, the hope of many REM clones imprisoned there, as well as, real people who go missing daily, and are trapped in the cloning centres.


We sincerely beg you.

Donald Marshall

# Appendices

## Appendix A: Thien Thanh Thi Nguyen (Tila Tequila) Transcript

**Link:** https://www.youtube.com/watch?v=7mRZ7ItF9ls&ab_channel=Astral7ight

00.00 – 1.10 min: You know what... since you f****** with my program darling Queen Elizabeth [II] and the paedophilia ring and the cloning centres, and the cloning centres. That's right darling the cloning centres. Parents listen to me right now, they are blocking me but that is quite alright. They are blocking me but that is quite alright. Because I have many, many other forces; I shall not say their names right now, but I have many big plans to expose all of you disgusting, sadistic f***s! Okay? That is all. I shall save that for another time. But, however, I shall REPEAT: that was just an introduction to the reptilian family, leading all the way back. They call themselves the "The Black Nobility". Now that is just one part of it; alright?

1.11 - 2.47 min:   The Black Nobility; the reptilian family; all the way back from ancient times; so which they think... they feel like they are the divine chosen ones... from whom may I ask? Definitely. Definitely not God. Our Creator of the world. Reptilians: they feed on blood; children; the paedophilia ring; recently busted. Oh! It has been going on for centuries. Parents listen to me carefully. I don't care if I'm cutting out. I will continue this and I am not alone on this battle. Believe THAT! Believe THAT! I am not alone on this battle. I started out alone but I am marching on with MILLIONS; okay? So sit your old a** down okay. Because you are gonna roll over, but it doesn't matter anyway because you are all ancestral f***s! Who interbreed... ancestral f*****g... and then... and then... Oh! Only going to talk about cloning those children and... oh! And all those many children's parents listen to me carefully.

2.48 - 4.24 min: Hundreds of missing children come up every year. You wonder... why? How? How could this be? And then there is so called CPS [Child Protection Services] or whatever they are called; they come and take your children, just, just for nothing; right? Not to discredit everybody, because not everybody is bad. I'm talking about the bad people. And they take your kids... they take them as this... they treat them like... I can't even say the word. It's disgusting, it's sadistic. They... they... they take your kids... they toss them out like little [inaudible] cause they are so f*****g... Pardon my French, but then again when I'm dealing with these evil cum-buckets I have no holy words coming out of my mouth, because these are the only words they resonate to. So therefore that's how I refer to them. Because they can only [inaudible] ...their masters whiplash on them with these [inaudible] words of cursing, vileness and slaving and that is not what the true God is; okay? The God of Hell...; Anyways...

4.25 – 5.30 min:  There are these CLONING CENTRES where they take your children and do sadistic things to them. I'm not even talking about child molestation here; not to mention; uh there is one of them that got caught, flying out to Florida; to meet up with a four year old little girl, to have sex with a four year old girl.  That's right. Google it because it is so highly sinful... We have commercials about... you know starving kids; you know save the starving kids and it is heartbreaking. We can have commercials about it... why? Because it is a horrible thing and people can have commercials about it. WHY do we not have commercials about... 'Daddy please don't, don't. Mommy please don't let daddy let daddy touch me?' – because it is disgusting! It is so disgusting; beyond sin that no one, NO ONE, can even make a commercial about that because that's how sinful it is.

5.31 – 7.19 min: Do you understand that? Do you understand how sinful that is? These people, I'm not even going to call them people; alright? They take your children; they not only molest them; men f*** them and make them shoot each other. They give them guns. It's either you shoot him or I'm gonna shoot you. They are... mind you, they are children. Children. Yes. I'm speaking out, because I... uh! Who else is doing this? You're all just [inaudible]... shame on you... And actually the most recent paedophilia... got taken down... WOW! How long did that take? Really?! Do you know how long this has been going on? *Sigh* Alright I'm gonna calm down... but as a parent and I love parents out there. My heart goes out to all the parents out there who have missing children. You know, we all pray for them; every day.  And I put on a bold face in public every day; because there needs to be someone strong, believe that. But my strength comes from somewhere... that I have a very vulnerable emotional side where I feel very strongly for these children and innocent people. So therefore I want to speak out.

7.20 – 9.10 min: I have and I have my passion too; and in the end you shall all know why I am so passionate about exposing every single one of these scumbags; okay? The truth shall prevail and you all will know why. So, as for you parents... ah... there are no words to describe. But let me just expose because you can't just... there is a point where you CANNOT just turn the other way. You know this stuff is going on; and you go 'Oh well... that's their problem. Let's just turn the other cheek.' How long are you going to turn the other cheek, until it happens to your own freaking children? When, when, when your own child; three years old, get's run out [kidnapped] and gets blasted right in the head with a gun... yeah... there's more to that people; okay? And I'm not just saying that coming from some... I mean, actually, mothers, fathers out there... If you found out... I'm sure you would do way worse than what I am just saying. I'm just using voc. I'm just annihilating them vocally. I'm sure the parents out there who find out what their children have gone through, their missing children. I am pretty positive more than just a vocal annihilation of these scumbags that do this to your children; okay?

9.11 – 10.32 min: So keep on turning the other cheek folks. Hey, go and turn the other cheek; you are with the others. I am not. I AM NOT. Like I said you... There is only two ways to go about this: you're either with us: the good guys, or you're with the others. There is no in-between. Cause if you are in-between, hiding like cowards, turning the other cheek; doing whatever; well then you are a freaking coward and you are just a sheep. And sheep end up dying because you know what you are owned by "The Others". So pick one: you're either one of us: the good guys or you're part of the others. That is simple as that! Two choices: good guys; bad guys. In-between you're dead because the bad guys are going to suck your soul out [transfer your consciousness to your REM driven clone] and do some sadistic stuff to you and watch, and make you watch while they [do] pretty sadistic stuff to your children as well.

10.33 – 11.33 min: Do you know why they love children? Because they are innocent souls; they're innocent... they're, they're the most innocent pure beings in this planet. They're not harmed by anything. They're new to the world; bright-eyed pure innocent children. That is why these disgusting paedophile and these clone rings; cloning centres; satanic rituals; Brownsville Texas... There are many other cloning centres where they take your children that go missing. And you wonder why? What happens to them? I'm sorry to break this to you but that is what happens. Now either do you want to know what happens to them or do you want to turn the other freaking cheek?

11.34 – 13.09 min: Tune into my next show. I'm gonna upload stuff; I have an arsenal ready to blow up! Okay. And I have reason behind this. You all should know my personal reason soon; but this has nothing to do with me right now. But know that I'm back, I'm back with a vengeance and I'm back with an army full of people around the world who are sick and tired of treated like animals; or quote, unquote "COWS". We all know what that means. For the outside world (the masses) we all know the term "sheep", sheeple. But for the insiders we know what the cows are don't we? You know what "The Others" like to do with the cows, right? They start to herd you in... and to... yeah...I'm gonna end it at that. And to all the parents, families and children out there, I love you so much. I... have to maintain composure, because that is what I do. That is all. Over and out.

# *Appendix B: MK Ultra*

**MK Ultra** *-noun:* [Manufacturing Killers Utilizing Lethal Tradecraft Requiring Assassinations] The goal of mind control, using MK Ultra technology is to program an individual to carry out any task against their will and self-preservation instinct, and to control the absolute behaviour and thought patterns of the individual.

Modern-day MK Ultra involves an implantable microchip which is inserted into a Mark 2 clone of the victim. Every thought, reaction, hearing and visual observation causes a certain neurological potential, spikes, and patterns in the brain and its electromagnetic fields, which can now be decoded by the implantable microchip into thoughts, pictures and voices. The thoughts, pictures and voices of the implanted Mark 2 clone (victim) can now be displayed visually and heard on any system capable of converting visual images, such as a television or a computer. These images are usually displayed on a giant screen at the cloning centre.

The purpose of MK Ultra is to elicit a specific conditioned response in a victim (desired by the programmer) to an otherwise neutral stimulus. In other words, through the process of "classical conditioning" (which involves learning a new behaviour via the process of association. In simple terms two stimuli are linked together to produce a new learned response in a person) the implanted Mark 2 REM duplicate clone (victim) is placed thorough many similar recurring scenarios which are experienced (or perceived) by the victim as "real", because the programmer manipulates the victim's audio and visual field, and continuously pairs the victim with the neutral stimulus, so that either a positive or negative conditioned response is elicited in the victim towards the neutral stimulus.

In other words an implanted victim can be placed in many recurring situations deemed as frightful, where a mystery stranger saves the victim from the frightful situation over and over again. The victim will now have positive associations towards the mystery stranger and therefore the conditioned response is now one of 'positive associations' (towards the mystery stranger who did not elicit such a reaction before).

MK Ultra techniques are administered through Mark 2 (sleep driven) clones. In other words classical conditioning happens when the person sleeps. Memory suppression technologies are also used in conjunction with MK Ultra technology, which enables the programmer to control certain memories the victim remembers. The use of memory suppression technologies and MK Ultra technology allows the programmer to reinforce behaviour and elicit specific conditioned responses (in an original).

Therefore, in our example above, when the original meets the mystery stranger in real life, the original (victim) will be predisposed to the mystery stranger and automatically 'feel safe' around this person and may even believe that he / she should 'date this mystery stranger' – depending on what was programmed; because the victim was conditioned to elicit such an emotional response towards the mystery stranger in his / her sleep as a Mark 2 REM driven clone through MK Ultra functionality.

MK Ultra can also be used to create zombified individuals who are programmed to murder and remember nothing of their crime afterward. MK Ultra (technology) can also be used to disrupt the memory of the original, discredit people through unusual behaviour, make the person insane or commit suicide and murder.

MK Ultra has much functionality. Furthermore, because of its video and audio projection functionality, MK Ultra can also be used to compose music. MK Ultra is capable of relaying the Mark 2 REM driven clone's subconscious and conscious mind as visual images and audio, projected onto a screen. Therefore thoughts, pictures and voices which have been experienced consciously and subconsciously in one's life can be displayed visually and audibly on a television or computer screen. The Mark 2 clone now has the option of harmonising these thoughts, pictures, and voices into a coherent order which produces music through the thought process of his or her imagination. See Jim Cristea (2009); Berkeley News (2011); UC Berkeley Campus Life (2011) CTForecaster (2013); nature video (2013) and Stromberg (2013) for examples and discussions and the capability of MK Ultra technology.

# *Appendix C: The Illuminati*

**Illuminati** *–noun:* A modern-day criminal organisation operated by reprobate (depraved, unprincipled and wicked person) criminals. Their main agenda: is to enslave the whole world through advanced concealed technologies.

Today's Illuminati trace their roots back to Professor Adam Weishaupt who found the Illuminati on 1st May 1776. Since the inception of the Illuminati the intent has always been, and remains: "to bring about a NEW World Order that writes God out of the picture and deifies [glorifies] Lucifer." This intent is still prevalent today. The following excerpt is derived from A. Ralph Epperson (1990) *The New World Order:*

> Weishaupt was a teacher of Cannon Law (law governing the affairs of a Christian Church, especially the law created or recognised by the Papal authority in the Roman Catholic Church) at the University of Ingolstadt in Bavaria, now part of Germany.
>
> He even told the world, in his writings, where he would conceal the Order: "None is fitter than the three lower degrees of Free Masonry; the public is accustomed to it, expects little from it, and therefore takes little notice of it." He felt that this secrecy would lead him to success because he felt no one would be able to break into it. He wrote: "Our secret Association works in a way that nothing can withstand ...."
>
> Weishaupt accepted the fact that all secret associations and secret orders had two doctrines, one concealed and reserved for the Masters... the other public ...." and the Illuminati was [and are to this day] a secret society with two doctrines.
>
> Professor Weishaupt, its founder, boasted of his organization's secrecy. He realized that this secrecy would enable them to decide the fate of nations and because their deliberations were secret, no outsider could interfere. He wrote: "The great strength of our Order lies in its concealment; let it never appear in its own name, but always covered by another name, and another occupation." Weishaupt later wrote about that secrecy in a letter to a fellow member of the Illuminati: "Nothing can bring this about [the new world order] but hidden societies. Hidden schools of wisdom are the means which will one day free men from their bonds [the "bonds" of religion] Princes and nations shall vanish from the earth." So the secret societies were created to bring the world to the new society known as the New World Order. The members of these organizations obviously feel that their goals are so noble that they may perform whatever tasks are required of them to bring that goal to fruition. This means that murder, plunder, and lying all become acceptable as long as these methods assist its members in obtaining their goal.
>
> Adam Weishaupt, the founder of the Illuminati, wrote over and over and over again, that "the ends justified the means." Weishaupt also told initiates to use whatever means, which included murder, to achieve the goals of the association that he was joining. And that the major goal of the Illuminati, was the destruction of all religion, including Christianity. That meant that if Christians physically stood in the way, they could be removed by simply murdering them. Weishaupt even went so far as to say that anyone not willing to take the life of another was unfit to join the Illuminati. He wrote the following in a letter to a fellow member in 1778: "No man is fit for our Order who is not ... ready to go to every length ...."
>
> Another reason, that Weishaupt felt that the Illuminati would succeed, was the fact that he was offering his members worldwide power. He felt that this inducement would enable him to draw into his organization only those who would do anything to satisfy that desire for power. He wrote: "The true purpose of the Order was to rule the world. To achieve this it was necessary for the Order to destroy all religions, overthrow all governments and abolish private property."

But his religion had a different base than the traditional religion: his was based upon a worship of reason: "... then will Reason rule with unperceived sway." "... Reason will be the only code of Man. This is one of our greatest secrets." "When at last Reason becomes the religion of man, then will the problem be solved." Weishaupt's dedication of his organization to "reason" makes some sense when the reader recalls that "reason" has been defined as the "unbridled use of man's mind to solve man's problems without the involvement of God." The Bible calls this "the fruit of the tree of the knowledge of good and evil." It was this knowledge that God wanted man not to have, and it was the promise made to man by Lucifer that man could have it by eating of "the fruit." In addition, Weishaupt's religion offered its believers a reward not offered by any other religion: worldwide power!

Weishaupt wrote: "The pupils [members of the Illuminati] are convinced that the Order will rule the world. Every member therefore becomes a ruler." Weishaupt's religion not only offered power to his believers, but he offered them something else not guaranteed by any other religion: worldly success. He said that once a candidate had achieved the exalted degree of Illuminatus Minor, the fourth of the thirteen inside his Order, his superiors would: "assist him [the member] in bringing his talents into action, and [would] place him in situations most favourable for their exertion, so that he may be assured of success." Finally, the goal of the Illuminati was "man made perfect as a god - without God."

The ideology of "man made perfect as a god –without God" still remains to this day, and it is practiced by today's Illuminati members. The above phrase is what ties in Luciferian worship and trans-humanism. Lucifer is idolised by Illuminati members as the deity who gave man 'knowledge' and therefore is worthy of worship; God, -according to Luciferians, -did not want man to have knowledge and therefore is despised by Luciferians. Ingrained in the trans-humanism doctrine is the believe that: 'man can become 'god' through science and technology and in turn overthrow the Creator of the universe: God'. See LawOfIdentity (2014) and Mark Dice (2014).

These are the basics of Luciferianism. Therefore everything which is natural or pertains to nature must be contended or destroyed by Luciferians. This is why Illuminati members endorse having sex with children, killing first born sons, and drink blood. All the above go against nature and according to the 'edicts of Lucifer': paedophilia makes the person committing the act younger (it doesn't, it is just an excuse to act perverse on children because they know children are vulnerable); killing your first born son gives you good luck and fortune in this life (so yes, some Luciferians have sacrificed their first bon sons); and Illuminati members believe drinking blood / cannibalism is a 'purifying agent' (although in reality it causes spongiform encephalitis (holes in the brain)).

Modern-day Illuminati members still retain the goal of its founder "to bring about a NEW World Order that writes God out of the picture and deifies [glorifies] Lucifer." Infiltration through secrecy, still remains their mode of operation, for the current Illuminati and therefore they have secretly infiltrated all the major religions on earth; government and education – where each successive generation is being dumb down; they have continually diminished the ability for individuals to own private property, or claim inheritance; divided people against each other to continually diminish patriotism; and have continually diminished family values.

They also compartmentalise their knowledge between members. Until I fully exposed the Illuminati, many people who have been REM clones at the cloning centre did not know they were in fact REM driven clones, and thought they were in the 5th Dimension; the astral plane; a singularity; the spiritual realm; Valhalla; quantum hopping; a time stutter etc. or whatever else the Illuminati told them.

Today's Illuminati members also meet in secret (just like the founding members) as REM driven clones, **when they go to sleep**. Furthermore, because Illuminati meetings are in secret and not many people know the exact location (because knowledge is compartmentalised) of the cloning centre; or the fact that their consciousness has been transferred to Mark 2 REM driven clone bodies at the cloning centre (and they are not in their original bodies); as well as the fact that unsuspecting civilians have their memories suppressed; the points mentioned above are the reasons the Illuminati believe 'they are all powerful and untouchable'; and as a consequence, today's Illuminati members do all the disgusting things they want, because they believe no outsider can interfere.

The ring leaders of the Illuminati today also believe "the ends justify the means". This is why they clone, torture, molest, murder, and rape unsuspecting civilians as REM driven clones in their sleep. The Illuminati of today offer their members incitements to go along with their agenda and not oppose them (or face death). Another popular method is to entice their target with many, many wonderful prospects, and have the target believe they are joining a noble and prosperous venture, so that the target fulfils the objectives of the Illuminati unknowingly; promoting the Illuminati in a positive way, because the target has been deceived to perceive the nature of the Illuminati as 'positive'; by the time the target finds out the true intent of the Illuminati, and the evil which emanates from it, it is too late. Those who rise up in the ranks of the Illuminati are the men and women who have an insatiable lust for power, and most importantly: the men and women who want to rule the world.

Modern-day Illuminati members also wish to become gods (through technology); overthrow the Creator, and achieve their overall aim of enslaving mankind. This is why they clone people, and clone people in high rank society from all walks of life (movie stars, musicians, politicians etc.; whether the person willing wants to be part of the Illuminati or not) so long as that person is in a position of power and influence, the Illuminati clone that person, and threaten that person, for example:- "Hey, you're going to hang with us –or else" –through such coercion, the people in high rank society who have power and influence will not oppose the Illuminati's plans to become gods; enslave mankind forever; and rule the world. Another reason for cloning high rank society is to include these people into the Illuminati (willingly or unwillingly) to ensure the world's populace remains in ignorance (because once all the world leaders and high rank society are cloned and under the coercion of the Illuminati nobody in a position of influence or power can warn the populace against the Illuminati) until the Illuminati's plan is completed and they have enslaved the world forever.

The Illuminati's overall aim of 'becoming gods' and ruling the world, as well as, mind controlling all the inhabitants of earth is also the reason the Illuminati:

- Administer drip feed disclosure through media, by telling some truths mixed with lies in order to conceal their true intentions and overall aim, and prevent the betrayed partner (the public) from ever discovering "the complete truth";
- Administer evaluative conditioning, by placing their symbols and ideology in popular media with positive associations, so that the unknowing and unsuspecting public will eventually become predisposed to the Illuminati and unsuspectingly have a positive or neutral response towards the Illuminati;
- Because they want to become 'gods' is also the reason the Illuminati is promoting RFID microchips and only discussing RFID microchips positively, while at the same time placing suppression (gagging) orders on anyone who speaks negatively about RFID microchips –which implies an unsuspecting public will willingly accept the microchip; and at the point of transaction, the person will have (unknowingly) given up their privacy to a third party (the Illuminati) for the rest of his / her life;
- Their aim to become 'gods' is also the reason the Illuminati are hurriedly trying to complete the HAARP grid across earth –because a complete HAARP grid will allow them to achieve their goal of mind control over the entire world; which fulfils their objective of becoming gods; because a complete HAARP grid will be capable of time travel, and therefore the Illuminati will be capable of going back to a previous time to correct the mistake(s) which led to their downfall; the Illuminati members will retain the knowledge of the previous time, and the rest of humanity will have no recollection of such a memory.

The Illuminati is **not** a joke. It is **not** fiction. They are very real, and part of humanity's reality; and through advanced concealed technologies the Illuminati aim to enslave humanity forever. The ring leaders of the present Illuminati includes Queen Elizabeth II, Prince Philip Duke of Edinburgh, Prince Charles of Wales and Vladimir Putin. I have also detailed the actions of the ringleaders in the main text in this disclosure, as well as, detailed other modern-day evil Illuminati members on my Facebook and Proboards. It is time the good people of earth, stopped being afraid, do the right thing, put a stop to this evil, and save themselves, as well as their children's children from being slaves forever. Spread and share this disclosure.

# Glossary

**Aneurysm** -*noun:* An excessive swelling of the wall of an artery at a fixed point in the body. A brain aneurysm is therefore a: bulge or ballooning in a blood vessel in the brain. It often looks like a berry hanging on a stem. A brain aneurysm can leak or rapture, causing bleeding into the brain.

**Brain Aneurysm** -*noun:* see Aneurysm.

**Clone** –*noun:* a cell, group of cells, an organism produced asexually from a single ancestor and is genetically identical to a single ancestor.

**Concealed Technology** -*noun:* hidden machinery and devices undisclosed and currently unavailable for public consumption. Concealed (or military) technology develops at a rate of 44 years for every 12 months which passes in comparison to the technology the public is currently accustomed to. Origin: Phil Schneider.

**Cloning Centre** –*noun:* a physical location (on earth) where duplicate and replicate clones are produced. These physical locations are usually Deep Underground Military Bases (DUMBs). DUMBs have an entire floor dedicated to cloning. It is also a place where Illuminati members meet with each other as REM driven clones. The above-ground cloning centre where many high profile people attend, can be found within a radius of 5/6 hours drive from the Robert Pickton Farm Port Coquitlam, British Columbia, in Canada, somewhere at a remote nature reserve.

**Cloning Technology** -*noun:* the technological advancements in medicine, science and technology used to produce duplicate and replicate copies of originals.

**Conditioned Response** -*noun:* an automatic response established by training to an ordinarily neutral stimulus.

**Conditioned Stimulus** –*noun:* A previously neutral stimulus that, after repeated association with an unconditioned stimulus, elicits the response produced by the unconditioned stimulus itself.

**Consciousness** –*noun:* the state of being aware of and responsive to one's surroundings; a person's awareness or perception of something.

**Consciousness Transfer** -*noun or verb:* the process of transferring or copying the mental content (including long-term memory and "self") from a particular brain and copying it to a computational device; artificial body or avatar body such as that of a robot or clone version of the original. It is also the feat in which the person's mental content (long term memory and "self") moves from one body into another.

**Depopulation** *verb:* to remove or reduce the population of, as by destruction or force.

**Drip Feed Disclosure** *noun or verb:* is the process of supplying information but in small amounts overtime. Drip feed disclosure is also the process of revealing information slowly overtime, possibly telling lies to conceal certain aspects of the truth until the source administering the drip feed disclosure has adequate time to let out the truth in a slow and controlled way, thereby delaying the betrayed partner (in this disclosure, the public) from having the "complete truth" for some time.

**DUMB** *–noun:* [Deep Underground Military Base] a facility directly owned and operated by or for the military or one of its branches that shelters military equipment and personnel, and facilitates training and operations beneath the surface of the earth.

**Duplicate Clone** *-noun:* a fully formed human body which is a genetic copy of original developed through the process of regenerative technology. Duplicate clones are grown in a big thick tank full of (salty) water.

**Duplication Cloning** *-verb:* involves agitating the cells of on an original repetitively until a fully formed human body of the original is developed. Duplicate clones take an average of 5 months to form into a fully developed human body of the original through the process of regenerative medicine and technology.

**Evaluative Conditioning** *-noun:* is a change in liking, which occurs due to an association with a positive or negative stimulus.

**H.A.A.R.P. Technology** *–noun:* [High frequency Active Auroral Research Program] a radio transmitting system that can bounce signals off the Earth's upper atmosphere, (60km (37 miles) to 1000km (620 miles) high) back to probe deep into the earth or sea. HAARP is also capable of: disrupting human mental processes; knocking out all global communication systems; changing weather patterns over large areas; interfering with wildlife and migration patterns; hurting ecosystems; negatively affect human beings health, moods and mental states; and unnaturally 'boil' the earth's upper atmosphere. HAARP used correctly will control the weather without any adverse effects.

**H.A.A.R.P. Grid** *–noun:* a network of radio transmitters which can bounce signals off the earth's upper surface. Each transmitter is located at a specific point across earth and communicates in unison with other radio transmitters across the earth. At this present time of writing, a HAARP grid has **not** been completed, although the Illuminati are working twice as fast to complete a HAARP grid. The threat to humanity once a HAARP grid is completed includes: mind control over the entire world's inhabitants. A completed HAARP grid will also be capable of time travel, and therefore the Illuminati will always be able to go back to a pervious point in time to correct the mistake(s) which led to their downfall. Humanity will be slaves forever.

**Habeas Corpus** *-noun:* is [A] writ [formal document] requiring a person under arrest to be brought before a judge or into court, especially to secure the person's release unless lawful grounds are shown for their detention.

**Heart Attack** *-noun:* A sudden occurrence of a blockage of the flow of blood to the heart.

**Human Clone** *–noun:* The creation of a genetically identical copy of a human.

**Ionosphere** –*noun:* the layer of the earth's atmosphere which contains a high concentration of ions and free electrons and is able to reflect radio waves. It lies above the mesosphere and extends from about 60km (37 miles) to 1,000 km (620 miles) above the earth's surface.

**Illuminati** –*noun:* A modern-day criminal organisation operated by reprobate (depraved, unprincipled and wicked person) criminals. Their main agenda: is to enslave the whole world through advanced concealed technologies. See Appendix C for further discussion.

**Mark 2 Clone** –*noun:* Is a sleep driven clone; specifically, a REM sleep driven clone. A Mark 2 Clone is activated by transferring the consciousness of an original into a Mark 2 Clone **only when** the original reaches REM sleep (usually 90 to 110 minutes **after** the original falls asleep). Once the consciousness of the original is transferred from the original's body to the Mark 2 Clone, the Mark 2 clone is now capable of motion: such as walking, talking etc. The Mark 2 clone 'drops limp' and becomes motionless once the original wakes up from sleep. The original's consciousness no longer resides in the Mark 2 clone (once the original is awake) and therefore the Mark 2 clone is now incapable of motion. Mark 2 Clones are also known as "REM Driven Clones" and "REM Duplicate Clones".

**Memory Suppression** –*noun or verb:* is the selective removal of memories or associations with the mind using memory suppression technology.

**Memory Suppression Technology** –*noun:* any scientifically advanced technology used selectively to remove memories from the conscious mind.

**Mind-Voice Technology** –*noun:* an advanced technology capable of reading, listening, hearing and broadcasting a person's inner voice or thoughts. It is capable of replicating sounds **exactly**. Therefore an individual can hear the sound of drums, a guitar or any instrument and replicate that sound exactly just by thinking about it. Consequently, Mind-voice technology has the functionality of producing music.

**Military Technology** –*noun:* machinery and devices developed from scientific knowledge used by the Armed Forces which advance at a rate of 44 years for every 12 months which passes, compared to the technology the public is accustomed to. Origin: Phil Schneider

**MK Ultra** -*noun:* [Manufacturing Killers Utilizing Lethal Tradecraft Requiring Assassinations] the goal of mind control, using MK Ultra technology is to program an individual to carry out any task against their will and self-preservation instinct and to control the absolute behaviour and thought patterns of the individual. See Appendix B for further details.

**Neutral Stimulus** –*noun:* is a stimulus which initially produces no specific response other than focusing attention. In classical conditioning, when used together with an unconditioned stimulus, the neutral stimulus becomes a conditioned stimulus.

**Negative Association** -*noun:* is an undesirable experience or perception.

**Negative Stimulus** -*noun:* a stimulus with undesirable consequences.

**New World Order** -*noun:* [NWO] Agenda. The whole NWO agenda is to turn humanity into mindless slaves forever; whereby the post-humans / trans-humans mind control the entire world's populace either through RFID microchips or a completed HAARP grid. Another aspect of the NWO agenda is to depopulate the world's current population of 7.3 billion people to 500 million people (and never exceed a world population of 500 million people afterwards); ruled by a one world government; a one world ruler; with a one world religion. See Appendix C for more details.

**Original** *–noun:* A person who is **not** a clone.

**Pain Receptor** -*noun:* Any one of the many nerve endings throughout the body that warn of harmful changes in the environment such as excessive pressure or temperature.

**Positive Association** -*noun:* is a desirable experience or perception.

**Positive stimulus** -*noun:* a stimulus with desirable consequences.

**Posthumanism** *–noun:* seeks to rewrite the very definition of being human. It is the condition in which humans and intelligent technology become intertwined. In the Posthuman there are no essential differences or absolute demarcations between bodily existence and computer stimulation, cybernetic mechanism and biological organism, robot technology and human goals.

**Posthuman** -*noun:* see Posthumanism.

**Project MK Ultra** -*noun:* see MK Ultra.

**Regenerative Medicine** -*noun:* (of a living organism) the process of re-growing new tissues after loss or damage.

**Regenerative Technology** -*noun:* any machinery or device developed from scientific knowledge which has the capability to re-grow new tissues after loss or damage.

**REM Sleep** *–noun:* [Rapid Eye Movement] is the fifth stage of sleep in the sleep cycle. It takes 90 to 110 minutes to reach REM sleep after we fall asleep. REM sleep is also known as the "period of paralysation". The involuntary muscles such as the brain become more active whereas voluntary muscles (those that you move by choice) such as your arms and legs become more relaxed or paralysed. REM sleep is a kind of sleep that occurs at intervals during sleep, and it is characterised by rapid eye movements.

**REM Driven Clone** -*noun:* [Rapid Eye Movement Driven Clone] a clone that can only become activated, once the original is in REM sleep. See Mark 2 Clone.

**REM Duplicate Clone** -*noun:* [Rapid Eye Movement Driven Clone] a clone developed by regenerative medicine and technology and is therefore an identical copy of an original. REM duplicate clones can only become activated when the original is in REM sleep. See Mark 2 Clone.

**REM Driven Clone Death** —*noun:* the process where an original dies because of constant torture to their REM driven clone or where a constant electrical current is applied to the REM driven clone resulting in death of an original usually in the form of an aneurysm or heart attack (because consciousness is linked) in the original's body.

**REM Driven Clone Torture** —*noun or verb:* the action or practice of inflicting serve pain on a REM driven clone. REM driven clone torture causes biological and physiological responses in the original's body because consciousness is linked. Intermittent REM driven clone torture (depending on what is done) causes the original to experience severe headaches, an upset stomach, achy limbs, sickness; a weakened heart. Continuous REM driven clone torture will lead to the death of the original; usually in the form of aneurysm or heart attack in the original's body.

**Replication Cloning** —*verb:* involves giving birth to a genetic identical of an original where the newborn starts life off as a baby and matures. The newborn is referred to as a clone.

**RFID Technology** -*noun:* [Radio Frequency Identification] are electronic microchips the size of a grain of sand that can be directly embedded into the human flesh. RFID microchips communicate wirelessly through the use of electromagnetic fields to transfer data. RFID microchips link the brains of people via the implanted microchip to satellites controlled by ground base super-computers. The dangers of RFID microchips to the implanted person are: total loss of privacy and total control of the person's physical body functions, mental and emotional thought processes, including the implanted person's subconscious or dreams –for the rest of that person's life! RFID microchips are also tracking devices, and the implanted person can be tracked anywhere on the globe.

**Selling One's Soul** -*verb:* to sell the use one's "Mark 2" REM driven clone to the Illuminati, for the Illuminati to use the individual's Mark 2 REM driven clone in whatever manner the Illuminati wishes. There are no returns once the individual has signed over his / her (soul) Mark 2 REM driven clone. When an individual sells their (soul) Mark 2 REM driven clone, the person has also entered into a contract to sell the Mark 2 REM driven clone(s) of their current children (if they have any) as well as any unborn children the person may have later in life. The person sells all their descendants (souls) Mark 2 REM driven clones to the Illuminati, once the individual sells their (soul) Mark 2 REM driven clone to the Illuminati. Selling one's (soul) Mark 2 REM driven clone is considered **a serious business transaction** to the Illuminati. There are no returns. If the person ever makes a fuss and wants their (soul) Mark 2 REM driven clone back, the Illuminati will either torture the person's Mark 2 Clone, or apply a constant electric current to the person's Mark 2 Clone until the person either has a heart attack or aneurysm in their original body. This is what public figures are hinting at when they say "They have sold their soul". They have sold the use of their Mark 2 REM driven clone to the Illuminati. Selling one's soul is not a joke. Never sell your soul.

**Stimulus** —*noun:* is something that causes a reaction, especially interest, excitement or energy. It is also an energy change registered by the senses. For example a stimulus can be a shinny object for a baby.

**Technology** —*noun:* machinery and devices developed from scientific knowledge.

**Technological Advancement** *–noun:* is incorporating, by means of experimental development, a characteristic or capability not previously existing or available in standard practice, into a new or existing process or product that enhances a product's performance. Novelty, uniqueness, or innovation alone does not indicate a technological advancement.

**Transhumanism** *–noun:* the belief or theory that the human race can evolve beyond its current physical and mental limitations, especially by means of science and technology.

**Unconditioned Response** *–noun:* is a response to a neutral stimulus we have no / little control over. It is a natural automatic response. For example, food is an unconditioned stimulus for a hungry animal, and salivation is the unconditioned response.

**Unconditioned Stimulus** *–noun:* A stimulus that elicits an unconditioned response.

**All references in this document have been saved and backed-up; therefore if any link in this document, is ever deleted, modified etc. (online), let me know.**

## *References*

2045 Initiative (2015) *2045 Strategic Social Initiative* [Online] Available from: http://2045.com/ [Accessed 1st June 2015]

Albrecht, K., and McIntyre (2005) *Spychips: How Major Corporations and Government Plan to Track Your Every Move with RFID.* Plume

Alford, J., (2014) *Scientist Selectively Erase and Restore Memories* [Online] Available from: http://www.iflscience.com/brain/scientists-selectively-erase-and-restore-memories [Accessed 8th July 2015]

Alford, J., (2015) *Scientist Implant False Memories Into Sleeping Mice* [Online] Available from: http://www.iflscience.com/brain/scientists-implant-false-memories-sleeping-mice [Accessed 28th July 2015]

Animal Research (1996) *Cloning Dolly the Sheep* [Online] Available from: http://www.animalresearch.info/en/medical-advances/timeline/cloning-dolly-the-sheep/ [Accessed 28th June 2014]

Anthony, S., (2012) *GoFlow: a DIY tDCS brain-boosting kit* [Online] Available from: http://www.extremetech.com/extreme/121861-goflow-a-diy-tdcs-brain-boosting-kit [Accessed 24th May 2015]

Anthony, S., (2013) *What is transhumanism, or, what does it mean to be human?* [Online] Available from: http://www.extremetech.com/extreme/152240-what-is-transhumanism-or-what-does-it-mean-to-be-human [Accessed 24th May 2015]

Astral 7sight (2013a) *Illuminati Exposed 2013: Chemtrails, Atlantis, Clones, Drones & Vril Part 1/8.* [Online video]. June 23rd 2013. Available from: https://www.youtube.com/watch?v=UonnFuHLJKc&ab_channel=Astral7ight [Accessed 12th July 2015]

Astral 7sight (2013b) *Illuminati Exposed 2013: Chemtrails, Atlantis, Clones, Drones & Vril Part 2/8.* [Online video]. June 23rd 2013. Available from: https://www.youtube.com/watch?v=QPAXCwu5MIo&ab_channel=Astral7ight [Accessed 12th July 2015]

Astral 7sight (2013c) *Illuminati Exposed 2013: Chemtrails, Atlantis, Clones, Drones & Vril Part 3/8.* [Online video]. June 23rd 2013. Available from: https://www.youtube.com/watch?v=5zlJ0VQP444&ab_channel=Astral7ight [Accessed 12th July 2015]

Astral 7sight (2013d) *Illuminati Exposed 2013: Chemtrails, Atlantis, Clones, Drones & Vril Part 4/8.* [Online video]. June 23rd 2013. Available from: https://www.youtube.com/watch?v=dCGhrDEl-q8&ab_channel=Astral7ight [Accessed 12th July 2015]

Astral 7sight (2013e) *Illuminati Exposed 2013: Chemtrails, Atlantis, Clones, Drones & Vril Part 5/8.* [Online video]. June 23rd 2013. Available from: https://www.youtube.com/watch?v=EDyerA-k8Ic&ab_channel=Astral7ight [Accessed 12th July 2015]

Astral 7sight (2013f) *Illuminati Exposed 2013: Chemtrails, Atlantis, Clones, Drones & Vril Part 6/8.* [Online video]. June 23rd 2013. Available from: https://www.youtube.com/watch?v=iqQZPpXl2yg&ab_channel=Astral7ight [Accessed 12th July 2015]

Astral 7sight (2013g) *Illuminati Exposed 2013: Chemtrails, Atlantis, Clones, Drones & Vril Part 7/8.* [Online video]. June 23rd 2013. Available from: https://www.youtube.com/watch?v=WYZSOnyWwP8&ab_channel=Astral7ight [Accessed 12th July 2015]

Astral 7sight (2013h) *Illuminati Exposed 2013: Chemtrails, Atlantis, Clones, Drones & Vril Part 8/8.* [Online video]. June 23rd 2013. Available from: https://www.youtube.com/watch?v=Y18m0gPLQhM&ab_channel=Astral7ight [Accessed 12th July 2015]

Astral 7sight (2013i) *Celebrity Tila Tequila: Missing Children and Cloning Centers* [Online video]. June 7th 2013. Available from: https://www.youtube.com/watch?v=7mRZ7ItF9ls&ab_channel=Astral7ight [Accessed 12th July 2015]

*Avatar* (2009) Film. Directed by James Cameron. [DVD]. UK: 20th Century Fox

BBC Future (2015) *BBC Future* [Online] Available from: http://www.bbc.com/future [Accessed 28th July 2015]

BBC Horizon (2009) *Why Do We Dream BBC Horizon* [Online video]. May 15th 2013. Available from: https://www.youtube.com/watch?v=E8MZ1twv0cU&ab_channel=AHOlearning [Accessed: 7th June 2015]

BBC News (2000) *Scientist 'clone' monkey* [Online] Available from: http://news.bbc.co.uk/1/hi/sci/tech/602027.stm [Accessed: 28th June 2015]

BBC News (2015a) *BBC News* [Online] Available from:
http://www.bbc.co.uk/news/science_and_environment [Accessed 28th July 2015]

BBC News (2015b) *BBC News* [Online] Available from:
http://www.bbc.co.uk/news/technology [Accessed 28th July]

BEAMS (2007) *BT's 'Soul Catcher2025' Implants* [Online] Available from:
http://www.beamsinvestigations.org/BT's%20'Soul%20Catcher%202025'%20Implants.htm
[Accessed 1st June 2015]

Begich, N., & Manning, J., (1997) *ANGELS DON'T PLAY THIS HAARP. Advances in Tesla Technology* [Online] Available from:
http://www.alachuacounty.us/Depts/epd/EPAC/Angels%20Dont%20Play%20This%20HAA
RP%20by%20Nick%20Begich%201997.pdf [Accessed 15th June 2015]

Berkeley News (2011) *Scientists use brain imaging to reveal the movies in our mind* [Online]
Available from: http://news.berkeley.edu/2011/09/22/brain-movies/ [Accessed: 22nd July
2015]

Beter, P., (2011) *"Organic Robotoids are real" by Dr Peter Beter* [Online video]. April 15th
2011. Available from:
https://www.youtube.com/watch?v=nc0m5UMPwtU&ab_channel=youlittlerocket [Accessed
6th July 2015]

Bloomberg Business (2015) *See Future of Artificial Intelligence in Mind Clones Right Now!*
[Online video] Available from:
https://www.youtube.com/watch?v=4bqZp9TPYVk&ab_channel=BloombergBusiness
[Accessed 27th June 2015]

Borghino, D., (2012) *"Avatar" project aims for human immortality by 2045* [Online]
Available from: http://www.gizmag.com/avatar-project-2045/23454/ [Accessed 3rd June
2015]

Boringest (2006) *Bush Video 10 years ago!* [Online video]. January 3rd 2006. Available from:
https://www.youtube.com/watch?v=pw4Bhmm22xo&ab_channel=boringest [Accessed: 11th
May 2015]

BritneySpearsVevo (2009) *Britney Spears –Break The Ice* [Online video] October 24th 2009.
Available from:
https://www.youtube.com/watch?v=eQFIKP9rGhQ&ab_channel=BritneySpearsVEVO
[Accessed 18th July 2015]

BritneySpearsVevo (2011) *Britney Spears –Hold it Against me* [Online video] February 17th 2011. Available from: https://www.youtube.com/watch?v=-Edv8Onsrgg&ab_channel=BritneySpearsVEVO [Accessed 18th July 2015]

Campbell, T., (2008) *Physics, Metaphysics and the nature of Consciousness* [Dr Thomas Campbell –My Big TOE (1 of 18)] [Online video] May 25th 2008. Available from: https://www.youtube.com/watch?v=MxECb7zcQhQ&list=PLBFFCEB1CAEDF9E6C&ab_channel=akn0ledge [Accessed 4th July 2015]

Carmichael, J., (2013) *Mouse Cloned From A Mere Drop of Blood* [Online] Available from: http://www.popsci.com/science/article/2013-06/mouse-cloned-mere-drop-blood [Accessed 19th July 2015]

CBS (2008) *Regeneration of Cells – Regrowing finger* [Online video] May 15th 2010. Available from: https://www.youtube.com/watch?v=ITxx2sOLW2Y&ab_channel=Weltenspur2 [Accessed: 25th June 2015]

Cherry, K., (2015) *What is Consciousness* [Online] Available from: http://psychology.about.com/od/statesofconsciousness/f/consciousness.htm [Accessed 1st July 2015]

CreativeForceVideo (2014) *Speaking with Nostradamus, Quantum Hypnosis with Delores Cannon* [Online video] August 2nd 2014. Available from: https://www.youtube.com/watch?v=CBOml6LTbpM&ab_channel=CreativeForceVideo [Accessed 25th July 2015]

Crystal Links (2015) *Nostradamus* [Online] Available from: http://www.crystalinks.com/nostradamus.html [Accessed 25th July 2015]

CTForecaster (2013) *Japanese Dream Recording Machine –Update* [Online video]. April 12th 2013. Available from: https://www.youtube.com/watch?v=gQueU9a8URw&ab_channel=CTForecaster [Accessed: 22nd July 2015]

Daily Mail Online (2015) *Mail Online* [Online] Available from: http://www.dailymail.co.uk/sciencetech/index.html [Accessed 28th July 2015]

De Houwer, J., Thomas, S., & Baeyens, F. (2001) *Associative Learning of Likes and Dislikes: A Review of 25 years of Research on Human Evaluative Conditioning.* Psychological Bulletin, Vol. 127, No.6, 853-869 In Hale, J., (2012) *What influences are Food Likes and Dislikes?* [Online] Available from: http://psychcentral.com/blog/archives/2012/02/15/what-influences-our-food-likes-and-dislikes/ [Accessed 28th June 2015]

Dictionary Reference (2015) *Consciousness* [Online] Available from: http://dictionary.reference.com/browse/consciousness?s=t [Accessed 30th June 2015]

Disclose TruthTV (2015) *Delores Cannon on WW3, Antichrist Nostradamus Prophecies [Full Video]* [Online video] March 19th 2015. Available from: https://www.youtube.com/watch?v=l0aCHrY0ObI&ab_channel=DiscloseTruthTV [Accessed 26th July 2015]

Donald Marshall Proboards (2015) *Donald Marshall Proboards* [Online] Available from: http://donaldmarshall.proboards.com/ [28th July 2015]

Ehrsson, H.H., (2013) *Inspirational Lecture –Professor Henrik Ehrsson* [Online video] October 3rd 2013. Available from: https://www.youtube.com/watch?v=iR7HissYN2U&ab_channel=karolinskainstitutet [Accessed 2nd July 2013]

Epperson, A. R., (1990) *The New World Order*, Publius Press. [Online] Available from: https://ia700406.us.archive.org/27/items/TheNewWorldOrder_342/TheNewWorldOrder.pdf [Accessed 7th July 2015]

Fox 4 News –Dallas Fort Worth (2014) *Aug. 15, 1988 – George W. Bush –KDFW* [Online video]. June 23rd 2014. Available from: https://www.youtube.com/watch?v=zwrl2axvPmY&ab_channel=FOX4News-Dallas-FortWorth [Accessed: 15th May 2015]

FW: Thinking (2014) *Erase and Restore your memories* [Online video]. Jun 18th 2014. Available from: https://www.youtube.com/watch?v=PpzzD_103jc&ab_channel=FW:Thinking [Accessed 8th July 2015]

Galactic (2012a) *Conversations With Nostradamus Volume One* [Online] Available from: http://galactic.no/rune/DoloresCannon_books/Dolores-Cannon-Conversations-With-Nostradamus-Volume-1.pdf [Accessed 25th July 2015]

Galactic (2012b) *Conversations With Nostradamus Volume Two* [Online] Available from: http://galactic.no/rune/DoloresCannon_books/Dolores-Cannon-Conversations-With-Nostradamus-V2.pdf [Accessed 25th July 2015]

Gizmag (2015) *Gizmag* [Online] Available from: http://www.gizmag.com/ [Accessed 28th July 2015]

Greenberg, P., (2013) *No More Bad Flashback: Scientist Find Gene That Erases Memories* [Online] Available from: http://mashable.com/2013/09/25/erase-bad-memories/ [Accessed 11th June 2015]

Hale, J., (2012) *What influences are Food Likes and Dislikes?* [Online] Available from: http://psychcentral.com/blog/archives/2012/02/15/what-influences-our-food-likes-and-dislikes/ [Accessed 28th June 2015]

Halliday, P., (2013) *Whistleblowing: the new 'public interest' test and other developments.* [Online] Available from: http://www.11kbw.com/uploads/files/PHPaper.pdf [Accessed 8th May 2015], p. 2

Hewitt, J., (2012) *How to create a mind or die trying* [Online] Available from: http://www.extremetech.com/extreme/141507-how-to-create-a-mind-or-die-trying [Accessed 24th May 2015]

History (2015) *George W. Bush* [Online] Available from: http://www.history.com/topics/us-presidents/george-w-bush [Accessed 14th May 2015]

*Hostel* (2006) Film. Directed by Eli Roth. [DVD]. USA:  Lionsgate

*Hostel: Part II* (2007) Film. Directed by Eli Roth. [DVD]. USA:  Lionsgate

*Hostel: Part III* (2011) Film. Directed by Scott Spiegel. [DVD]. USA:  Sony Pictures Home Entertainment

*Inception* (2010) Film. Directed by Christopher Nolan. [DVD]. UK:  Warner Bros. Pictures

inifiniLor (2013) *Appeal from Survivors of Canadian Genocide* [Online video]. April 8th 2013. Available from: https://www.youtube.com/watch?v=cVYkctM1k90&ab_channel=infiniLor [Accessed 13th July 2015]

Jeanice Barcelo (2013) *BNE Radio Show w/ guest Donald Marshall* [Online video]. March 9th 2013. Available from: https://www.youtube.com/watch?v=3uzgu4ekT3c&ab_channel=JeaniceBarcelo [Accessed 11th July 2015]

Jim Cristea (2009) *Mind Reading - FMRI - Machine that Reads Your Thoughts - 60 Minutes* [Online video]. January 9th 2009. Available from: https://www.youtube.com/watch?v=Cwda7YWK0WQ&ab_channel=JimCristea [Accessed: 22nd July 2015]

Jones, A., (2008) *Reflections and Warnings: An Interview with Aaron Russo* [Online video]. June 1st 2009. Available from: https://www.youtube.com/watch?v=YGAaPjqdbgQ&ab_channel=rohstyles23 [Accessed: 12th May 2015]

KafkaWinstonWorld (2014) *IS THIS WHERE WE ARE GOING? THIS MOVIE WILL BLOW YOUR F%$NG MIND(mirrored)* [Online video]. December 11th 2014. Available from: https://www.youtube.com/watch?v=4mUII1HcsRg&ab_channel=KafkaWinstonWorld [Accessed 15th July 2015]

Kim, M., (2013) *MIT scientists implant a false memory into a mouse's brain* [Online] Available from: http://www.washingtonpost.com/national/health-science/inception-mit-scientists-implant-a-false-memory-into-a-mouses-brain/2013/07/25/47bdee7a-f49a-11e2-a2f1-a7acf9bd5d3a_story.html [Accessed 28th July 2015]

LawOfIdentity (2014) *"We Will Become Gods"* [Online video]. August 20th 2014. Available from: https://www.youtube.com/watch?v=5MmXHMaati0&ab_channel=LawOfIdentity [Accessed 23 July 2015]

Legal-dictionary (2015) *Habeas Corpus* [Online] Available from: http://legal-dictionary.thefreedictionary.com/habeas+corpus [Accessed 14th May 2015]

Mark Dice (2014) *Top Transhumanist Claims He Will Become God and Kill Anyone Who Tries to Stop Him!!!* [Online video] May 14th 2014. Available from: https://www.youtube.com/watch?v=KPJARo-5VXE&ab_channel=MarkDice [Accessed 24th July 2015]

Medical News Today (2015) *Paranoid Schizophrenia: Causes, Symptoms and Treatments* [Online] Available from: http://www.medicalnewstoday.com/articles/192621.php [Accessed 21st July 2015]

Megadeth (2001) *The World Needs a Hero* [CD] USA: Sanctuary Records Group Ltd

MK Ultra Compendium (1980) *Secret CIA Human Experiments in the United States: MK Ultra Mind Control Research Program.* [online video] May 26th 2012. Available from: https://www.youtube.com/watch?v=c4f9Hs0s1jQ&ab_channel=TheFilmArchives [Accessed: 22nd June 2015]

Mind-Computer (2012) *Synthetic telepathy "Artificial Telepathy"* [Online] Available from: http://mind-computer.com/2012/05/15/synthetic-telepathy-artificial-telepathy/ [Accessed 22nd June 2015]

Moss, S., (2009) *Evaluative conditioning* [online] Available from: http://www.psych-it.com.au/Psychlopedia/article.asp?id=312 [Accessed 28th June 2015]

Motherboard (2015) *Motherboard* [Online] Available from: http://motherboard.vice.com/en_uk [Accessed 28th July 2015]

MrCowShedder (2012) *Royal Babylon by Heathcote Williams (rough cut).* [Online video]. May 11th 2012. Available from: https://www.youtube.com/watch?v=jIukrdRhnpw&ab_channel=MrCowshedder [Accessed 14th July 2015]

MurdokDubstep (2010) *Where'd You Go – Fort Minor (Murdok Dubstep Remix)* [Online video]. July 22nd 2010. Available from: https://www.youtube.com/watch?v=7VdAvIf1Nc4&ab_channel=MurdokDubstep [Accessed 15th July 2015]

nature video (2013) *Reading minds* [Online video]. October 23rd 2013. Available from: https://www.youtube.com/watch?v=z8iEogscUl8&ab_channel=naturevideo [Accessed: 22nd July 2015]

New Scientist (2014) *Brain Decoder can eavesdrop on your inner voice* [Online] Available from: https://www.newscientist.com/article/mg22429934-000-brain-decoder-can-eavesdrop-on-your-inner-voice/ [Accessed 12th June 2015]

New Scientist (2015) *New Scientist* [Online] Available from: https://www.newscientist.com/ [Accessed 28th July 2015]

Non Mirage Truth Vision (2015) *CIA's Heart Attack Gun* [Online video]. Available from: https://www.youtube.com/watch?v=Uwy56QTV4cs&ab_channel=NonMirageTruthVision [Accessed 16th July 2015]

Open Minds (2011) *Phil Schneider's incredible ET claims.* [Online] Available from: http://www.openminds.tv/phil-schneiders-incredible-et-claims/9982 [Accessed 9th May 2015]

Paye, J-C., (2013) *The Suspension of Habeas Corpus in America* [Online] Available from: http://www.globalresearch.ca/the-suspension-of-habeas-corpus-in-america/5311701 [Accessed 20th May 2015]

Petkova, V. I., and Ehrsson, H.H., (2008) *If I Were You: Perceptual Illusion of Body Swapping,* PLoS ONE, Volume 3, Issue 12, pp. 1-9

Prigg, M., (2014) *Mindreading software could eavesdrop on your secret inner voice* [Online] Available from: *http://www.dailymail.co.uk/sciencetech/article-2814896/The-mindreading-machine-listen-voices-head-let-paralysed-speak-again.html* [Accessed 13th June 2015]

Project Camelot (2008a) *Project Camelot Interviews George Green – Part 1 of 2* [Online video]. April 16th 2008. Available from: https://www.youtube.com/watch?v=sSYXrWIA618&ab_channel=ProjectCamelot [Accessed: 11th May 2015]

Project Camelot (2008b) *Project Camelot Interviews George Green – Part 2 of 2* [Online video]. April 16th 2008. Available from: https://www.youtube.com/watch?v=6zSrg0IxHzI&ab_channel=ProjectCamelot [Accessed: 11th May 2015]

RainmanJhof (2011) *Boondox-Abadon* [Online video]. October 31st 2011. Available from: https://www.youtube.com/watch?v=C2bH4B5_83Q&ab_channel=RainmanJhof [Accessed 15th July]

Radar Online (2013) *Princess Dianna 'Killed By Bright Light Shone By Special Forces Soldiers Into Car She Was In'* [Online] Available from: http://radaronline.com/exclusives/2013/09/princess-diana-killed-died-death-forces-light-special-air-service/ [Accessed 17th July 2015]

Rense (2001) *Microchip Mind Control, Implants and Cybernetics* [Online] Available from: http://www.rense.com/general17/imp.htm [Accessed 20th June 2015]

Rense (2011) *Possible HAARP Locations Around the World* [Online] Available from: http://www.rense.com/general92/haarp.htm [Accessed 20th July 2015]

Russo, A., (1996) *Mad as Hell* [Online video]. May 10th 2011. Available from: https://www.youtube.com/watch?v=Zz4TI75MszQ&ab_channel=XRepublicTV [Accessed: 13th May 2015]

Russo, A., (2006) *Freedom to Fascism* [Online video]. May 10th 2011. Available from: https://www.youtube.com/watch?v=uNNeVu8wUak&ab_channel=RevolutionistsUnited [Accessed: 12th May 2015]

RT (2014) *Revolutionary way to 'switch off' pain discovered* [Online] Available from: http://www.rt.com/news/210031-revolutionary-painkiller-discovered-scientists/ [Accessed 19th July 2015]

RT (2015) *Living forever as a robot? Prototype lets humans upload their mind into mechanised 'heads'* [Online] Available from: http://www.rt.com/usa/229811-mind-clones-robot-afterlife/ [Accessed 27th June 2015]

SadSongs4You (2010) *Elton John –Candle In The Wind. With lyrics* [Online video]. August 23rd 2010. Available from: https://www.youtube.com/watch?v=80rHyABCb20&ab_channel=SadSongs4You [Accessed 17th July 2015]

Schechtman (2012) *The Story of my (Second) Life: Virtual Worlds and Narrative Identity,* Philosophy and Technology, Volume 25, Issue 3, pp. 329-343

Schneider, P., (1995) *Phil Schneider Documentary of truth about Aliens & UFO's & our Government.* [Online video]. September 21st 2013. Available from: https://www.youtube.com/watch?v=Oljrjxnixtw&ab_channel=AliensAmongUs [Accessed: 10th May 2015]

Schneider, P., (1996) *Phil Schneider's Last Speech ~ Two Months Before His Assassination ~ Aliens & Underground Bases* [Online video]. November 24th 2013. Available from: https://www.youtube.com/watch?v=Slgb5U-OqFM&ab_channel=FallofMedia [Accessed: 10th May 2015]

Science Channel (2014) *How to Grow a New Fingertip | World's Strangest.* [Online video] June 16th 2014. Available from: https://www.youtube.com/watch?v=DtBUM51t4iw&ab_channel=ScienceChannel [Accessed 23rd June 2015]

Science Daily (2014) *'Off switch' for pain discovered: Activating the adenosine A3 receptor subtype is key to powerful pain relief* [Online] Available from: http://www.sciencedaily.com/releases/2014/11/141126132639.htm [Accessed 19th July 2015]

Sheen, M., Begich, N., & Robbins, W., (2005) *Holes in Heaven? H.A.A.R.P. & Advances in Tesla Technology* [Online video]. October 8th 2014. Available from: https://www.youtube.com/watch?v=SWVU6DKcjyA&ab_channel=documentary2014 [Accessed: 15th June 2015]

SimpleGirl4ewer (2007) *Britney Spears – Mona Lisa* [Online video]. March 18th 2007. Available from: https://www.youtube.com/watch?v=xEecXKUxl1s&ab_channel=SimpleGirl4ewer [Accessed 18th July 2015]

Sleepdex (2015) *Stages of Sleep* [Online] Available from: http://www.sleepdex.org/stages.htm [Accessed: 5th June 2015]

*Star Wars Episode III: Revenge of the Sith* (2005) Film. Directed by George Lucas. [DVD]. USA: 20 Century Fox

Stromberg, J., (2013) *Scientist Figure Out What You See While You're Dreaming* [Online] Available from: http://www.smithsonianmag.com/science-nature/scientists-figure-out-what-you-see-while-youre-dreaming-15553304/?no-ist [Accessed 22nd July 2015]

*The 6th Day* (2000) Film. Directed by Roger Spottiswoode. [DVD]. USA: Columbia Pictures

The Guardian (2015a) *The Guardian* [Online] Available from: http://www.theguardian.com/science [Accessed 28th July 2015]

The Guardian (2015b) *The Guardian* [Online] Available from: http://www.theguardian.com/uk/technology [Accessed 28th July 2015]

The Independent (2015a) The Independent [Online] Available from: http://www.independent.co.uk/news/science/ [Accessed 28th July 2015]

The Independent (2015b) The Independent [Online] Available from: http://www.independent.co.uk/life-style/gadgets-and-tech/ [Accessed 28th July 2015]

*The Island* (2005) Film. Directed by Michael Bay. [DVD]. USA: DreamWorks Pictures

*The Manchurian Candidate* (2004) Film. Directed by Jonathan Demme. [DVD]. USA: Paramount Pictures

TheNanoAge (2015) *Transhumanism and Posthumanism: The Future of Us (Humanity Plus)* [Online] Available from: *http://www.thenanoage.com/transhumanism-posthumanism.htm#transhuman* [Accessed: 30th May 2015]

Truthstream (2006) *Rigged USA Elections Exposed.* March 2nd 2006. Available from: https://www.youtube.com/watch?v=JEzY2tnwExs&ab_channel=truthstream [Accessed: 22th May 2015]

UC Berkeley Campus Life (2011) *Vision Reconstruction* [Online video]. December 11th 2011 Available from: https://www.youtube.com/watch?v=6FsH7RK1S2E&feature=youtu.be&ab_channel=UCBerkeleyCampusLife [Accessed 22nd July 2015]

Vincent Eastwood (2013) *Illuminati Cloning Programs, Sex and Murder Cults and Reptilians! 26Feb2013* [Online video] February 26th 2013. Available from: https://www.youtube.com/watch?v=M_1UiFeV5Jg&ab_channel=VincentEastwood [10th July 2015]

Walcutt, D. L., (2013) *Stages of Sleep.* [Online] Available from: http://psychcentral.com/lib/stages-of-sleep/ [Accessed 5th June 2015]

Walther, E., Nagengast, B., & Trasselli, C., (2005). *Evaluative conditioning in social psychology: Facts and speculations.* Cognition and Emotion, 19, 175–196 In Moss, S., (2009) *Evaluative conditioning* [online] Available from: http://www.psych-it.com.au/Psychlopedia/article.asp?id=312 [Accessed 28th June 2015]

WhiteLiesVevo (2010) *White Lies – Bigger Than Us* [Online video]. November 18th 2010 Available from: https://www.youtube.com/watch?v=JW0yynlDmqQ&ab_channel=WhiteLiesVEVO [Accessed 18th July]

Winter, L., (2014) *Scientist Erase Memories with Light* [Online] Available from: http://www.iflscience.com/brain/scientists-erased-memories-light [Accessed 10th June 2015]

WorldTruth (2014) *The Georgia Guidestones* [Online] Available from: http://worldtruth.tv/the-georgia-guidestones-2/ [Accessed 16th May 2015]

YesEthan (2013) *Consciousness Science Kept Hidden* [Online Video] January 12th 2013. Available from: https://www.youtube.com/watch?v=LFSRTsLOiv0&ab_channel=YesEthan [Accessed 4th July 2015]

# *Legislation*

Computer Misuse Act (1990) Section 3A, *Making, supplying or obtaining articles for use in offence under section 1 or 3* [Online] Available from: http://www.legislation.gov.uk/ukpga/1990/18/section/3A [Accessed 8th May 2015]

Enterprise and Regulatory Reform Act (2013) Section 17, *Disclosures not protected unless believed to be made in the public interest.* [Online] Available from: http://www.legislation.gov.uk/ukpga/2013/24/section/17/enacted [Accessed 8th May 2015]

Employment Rights Act (1996) Section 43B, *Disclosures qualifying for protection.* [Online] Available from: http://www.legislation.gov.uk/ukpga/1996/18/section/43B [Accessed 8th May 2015]

Public Interest Disclosure Act (1998) Section 43B, *Disclosures qualifying for protection.* [Online] Available from: http://www.legislation.gov.uk/ukpga/1998/23/section/1 [Accessed 8th May 2015]

Serious Crime Act (2015) Section 41 3ZA, *Unauthorised acts causing, or creating risk of, serious damage.* [Online] Available from: http://www.legislation.gov.uk/ukpga/2015/9/section/41/enacted [Accessed 8th May 2015]

Printed in Great Britain
by Amazon